THE BEST OF KIN HUBBARD

KIN HUBBARD, ABOUT 1910

THE BEST OF KIN HUBBARD

ABE MARTIN'S

Sayings and Wisecracks,

———————

Abe's Neighbors, His Almanack,

Comic Drawings

EDITED AND INTRODUCED BY DAVID S. HAWES

Indiana University Press / *Bloomington and Indianapolis*

First paperback edition 1995

Library of Congress Cataloging in Publication Data
Hubbard, Kin, 1868–1930.
    The best of Kin Hubbard.

    Includes bibliographical references.
    I. Hawes, David S.   II. Title.
PS3515.U1413A6   1984   741.5'973   84–47704
ISBN 0-253-10611-7
ISBN 0-253-21007-0 (pbk.)

2 3 4 5 00 99 98 97 96 95

To The Family
All exuberant laughers

"Gramps" Bill Davies,
Wife Betty,
Bill, Rob, Maile, Dena

Contents

PREFACE

The American humorist Frank McKinney Hubbard (1868–1930) was born and raised in Bellefontaine, Ohio, but for about thirty wondrously productive years he lived and worked in Indianapolis, Indiana. In May of 1932, to signalize the acclaim that he had brought to his adopted state and the affection he had won within its borders and far beyond, the State of Indiana dedicated Brown County State Park as a memorial to Kin Hubbard. And to perpetuate remembrance of Abe Martin, Kin Hubbard's chief comic character, rustic Abe Martin Lodge, constructed of native hardwoods and Brown County stone, was built on a high ridge in the Park. A large framed photograph of handsome Kin Hubbard was hung over the stone fireplace in the lounge of the Lodge and in a sunny room just off the lounge a fascinating collection of Kin's books and drawings and a variety of memorabilia were exhibited. Cabins snugly set in the woods around the Lodge were named for Abe's "neighbors"—Fawn Lippincut, Constable Newt Plum, Uncle Niles Turner, and the others. The spacious stone-floored porch overlooks a striking panorama of the rugged, forested hills of Brown County.

Before he died in 1930, Kin Hubbard knew that Brown County State Park would commemorate his life and his work as a humorist. Always genuinely modest, he was humbled by the thought, but grateful and pleased. Brown County, Abe Martin, and Abe's neighbors had bestirred his imagination for many years, and he knew well the real territory that he peopled with fictitious characters. In the 1920s, especially in autumn, the Hubbards frequently were in Nashville, Indiana, situated at the edge of the thousands of wooded acres later to become Brown County State Park. Kin Hubbard made good friends in Nashville, relished listening by the hour to palaver in the General Store, traveled the length and breadth of Brown County, knew most of the roads and little villages: Hornettown Road, Possum Trot Road, Gnaw Bone, Story, Bean Blossom. Back then, of course, not everyone accepted congenially all of Abe Martin's wisecracks about Brown County folks. Some citizens bridled, felt offended. Possibly a few old-timers still feel thataway. On the other hand, some folks in Brown County, thoroughly caught up in Kin's fanciful world, tried to identify his characters among local people: "So and so [I won't mention names] is certainly the feller he had in mind for Abe Martin, and so and so fits Fawn Lippincut to a T." But all of this was many, many years ago.

Abe Martin has now become a vague, legendary folk figure to many people in Brown County; only a few now know the story behind the ubiquitous image. The photograph of Kin Hubbard is still at Abe Martin Lodge, as are many interesting samples of his creativity, but information about his life and accomplishments is sparse. Passing time and changing circumstances have almost obliterated knowledge about Kin Hubbard and Abe Martin, even in Brown County.

High time, then, to recount Kin Hubbard's story and restore to the world a generous fund of Abe Martin's laughter. It seems arrogant, however, to say that what is gathered here is *the* best of Kin Hubbard's humor. Better, rather, to say that here is what seems to be some of his most effective, relevant, and compelling work. Choice of much of the material here has been determined by audience responses to my presentation of Kin Hubbard's humor (in my performance as Abe Martin) to diverse assemblages in a variety of situations throughout Indiana and elsewhere in the country. Audience response, however, is not an infallible test for the effectiveness and durability of humor, for humor is essentially a perishable commodity. It can stay fresh and enticing for long periods, but it can also spoil immediately. And the things that people will or will not laugh at can change from period to period, even from day to day. I bear witness that during the twenty years that I have known Abe Martin some of Abe's sayings have moved into and out of favor with disconcerting frequency and speed. So, yes, some of Kin Hubbard's humor finally has perished, and many once-barbed sayings now seem corroded, dull. A portion of his humor is leading a precarious in-and-out existence. But I judge that a great deal of Kin Hubbard's work has tenaciously survived and may live on for a decent time in the future. Herein is a liberal helping of such comic fare. I hope you thoroughly enjoy it. If you do, hurry on back for more.

With joy—and relief—I end a task that has been many, many years adoing. But I count every minute well spent if somehow I arouse renewed understanding and appreciation of Kin Hubbard and his laughter.

I now gladly acknowledge some of the indispensable help I have had along the way. My sincere thanks to Hubert C. Heffner and Robert G. Gunderson for their past and present wise guidance and hardy support; to Thomas E. Hubbard and Virginia Hubbard Schotters for their encouragement, and, additionally, to Tom Hubbard for the loan of invaluable primary materials; to Lilly Library for special assistance; to Tom Bertolacini of Bloomington Photo Lab for his excellent work on illustrations; to all those at Indiana University Press who really made the book read right, look right; to my wife, Betty, without whose constant expert help little, if anything, would be finished.

David S. Hawes

PART ONE

The Life and Career of
Frank McKinney Hubbard

(1868–1930)

Musings about the Life and Career of the American Humorist Kin Hubbard, Interlarded with Some of the Best of Abe Martin's Sayings

What Happened and What Followed After

It happened on December 17, 1904. In the annals of laughter in America the event surely must be joyfully commemorated. On that date Kin Hubbard's clownlike rustic character, Abe Martin, first began to talk horse sense and nonsense from the back page of the *Indianapolis News*. Frank McKinney (Kin) Hubbard, at that time a talented but little-known caricaturist working for the *News*, certainly had little confidence that Abe Martin would ever amount to much. But six days each week for twenty-six years, Kin continued to write a couple of unrelated witty-wise or nonsensical "sayings" for his rural sage. By December 1930, when Abe finally fell silent, millions of Americans each day eagerly turned the pages of their newspapers—some three hundred newspapers throughout the country—to see what Abe had to say for them to laugh about and think about that day. Abe Martin had become one of the most popular, profound, and comical cracker-barrel philosophers this country has ever known.

One of Kin Hubbard's fellow workers at the *Indianapolis News* called him a "genial Dapper Dan with the soul of an imp." And Kin was an imp—a keen, sharply observant, bunk-hating, and sometimes audacious imp, who loved to laugh, and who loved to make other folks laugh and think. Abe Martin had been dealing in truth and going after "make-believers and shams with a good stout hickory" for about six years when George Ade, the well-known Hoosier humorist, said that Kin Hubbard's "comments on men and affairs prove him to be a grim iconoclast, an analytical philosopher, and a good deal of a cut-up."[1] Abe Martin's subsequent rise to national prominence and popularity as a comic character and Kin Hubbard's consequent maturation as a significant American humorist present an engaging story.

When a feller says, "It hain't th' money, but th' principle o' th' thing," it's the money. It's no disgrace t' be poor, but it might as well be.

Growing Up in Bellefontaine

Kin Hubbard was born September 1, 1868, in the small agricultural town of Bellefontaine in Logan County, Ohio. Kin's father, Thomas Hubbard, was editor and publisher of a commendable country newspaper, the weekly *Bellefontaine Examiner.* The father, vigorous, independent, blessed with literary talent of a high order, was capable of doing all of the tasks involved in publishing a small-town weekly newspaper. But fortunately for him, as his large family grew up most of the children chose to take over key positions on the *Examiner* and make a career of journalism.

Kin Hubbard was the youngest in a family of six children. Unlike his two sisters and two of his older brothers, however, he never became heavily involved with the family newspaper. But he did work

Courtesy of the *Indianapolis News*

The artist, Kin Hubbard, 's so keerless
He draws Abe 'most eyeless and earless;
But he's never yit pictured him cheerless
　Er with fun 'at he tries to conceal . . .

　　　　James Whitcomb Riley

enough on the paper to learn the fundamentals of publishing a news-paper, and his intimate knowledge of typical country newspapers in-spired some of his best work as a humorist. Early on, for example, he realized the comic possibilities in a parody of "personals," that promi-nent feature of most small-town weeklies. So he invented many say-ings for Abe Martin that read like personals from a country newspaper:

> Young Lafe Bud went out huntin' with four other fellers Satur-day an' succeeded in shootin' three o' them when he was overtaken by darkness. Tipton Bud has sent his wife a souvenir pustal card from th' Yellowstone Park sayin', "I'm standin' right on th' edge o' a precipice lookin' straight down five thousand feet. Wish you wuz here."

Kin Hubbard's mother, Sarah Miller Hubbard, pert, witty, compas-sionate, was a devoted wife and mother who happily carried out the traditional responsibilities of a woman in the home. Both the mother and father were delighted at the early sprouting of Kin's skill as a silhouettist. At an early age, even before he started school, and about as soon as he could manipulate scissors, Kin could cut paper into like-nesses of people or animals. As if surprised at his precocious skill, Kin later said that he "could cut out from blank paper any kind of an animal with a correctness and deftness that was almost creepy."[2] Thus when still very young, Kin displayed keen observation and an unusual ability to coordinate the hand and eye, a fundamental skill essential to the work of a portrait artist or caricaturist. And somewhat later, when he was ten or eleven and had learned to draw, he substituted a pencil or pen and ink for scissors and found that his hand-eye coordination worked as well for him in doing drawings as in making silhouettes. Soon after he learned to draw, a strong comic element crept into much that he did with pencil or with pen and ink.

We know little about Kin Hubbard's educational experience in the elementary schools of Bellefontaine. But he did quit school at the age of thirteen before he had finished the seventh grade. There are indi-cations that he was a bright enough student but little stimulated or challenged in the classroom. Kin simply says: "School didn't interest me much and when I was in one of the early grades I retired for the purpose of taking a job in a paint shop."[3]

One can only surmise why Kin was unhappy and disinterested in school. But out of school he was an active, very happy boy. The tow-ering excitement of a circus in town, for example, fired Kin's imagina-tion and compelled him to stage his own "mah-vel-ous" circus acts in the Hubbards' spacious back yard. His exuberant love of everything about the circus persisted throughout his life. He was especially fond of the persona and antics of the clowns, and there is much about the character of Abe Martin that seems to celebrate Hubbard's durable fondness for circus clowns.

Another event joyously greeted by Kin Hubbard as a boy was the annual Logan County Fair, held in Bellefontaine each fall. There was always much that was exciting to see at the fair, to revel in and to remember. Best of all, perhaps, were those big Shanghai roosters and the other prize animals which inspired Hubbard to draw his animal caricatures. His ludicrous drawings of farm animals must be counted among his most effective laugh-fetching work as a caricaturist.

ABE MARTIN INSPECTS A CRITTER
AT THE COUNTY FAIR

When Kin Hubbard left school he kept busy and earned money doing odd jobs around Bellefontaine. With some of the first money he thus earned he bought costume items useful for an actor onstage or offstage: a plaid cape overcoat, a derby hat, and a cane. Thus early in his teens Kin began to nourish an interest in the theatre and in acting by secretly playing the role of an actor offstage. And during the teenage years he became an avid theatregoer. He established good terms with the manager of the Bellefontaine Grand Opera House and volunteered to do whatever the manager wanted in return for a pass to all the stage shows that came to town. Attending performances at the Opera House became vivid, wondrous experiences for Kin and remained luminous in his memory. So Kin early in life kept edging closer to a resplendent vision of himself as a professional actor.

When Kin was about sixteen, a number of things happened that promised to give new direction and meaning to his life. Thomas Hubbard gave his youngest son a set of engraver's tools, hoping that Kin would further develop his talent as an artist. Kin soon had a chance to test his skill as an engraver. In 1884, at the Republican National Convention, James G. Blaine and John H. Logan were nominated as candidates for President and Vice-President to run against Democrats Grover Cleveland and Thomas H. Hendricks. Kin made a wood-block engraving that caricatured Blaine and Logan, from which his father fashioned a cut that he published in the *Examiner*. This was Kin's first published caricature of politicians. It was a good beginning. Many years later he was to execute and publish caricatures of hundreds of politicians. The Hubbard family was jubilant about Kin's accomplishments as an engraver and caricaturist; "From that time on I was regarded as a natural born artist and everybody said that something ought to be done with me," he later remarked.

Indirectly the Democratic presidential victory of 1884 affected Kin Hubbard's life in another significant way. With the Democratic party once again in power under the leadership of President Grover Cleveland, Thomas Hubbard's lengthy and formidable defense of the Democratic party in Bellefontaine was recognized and rewarded. He was made postmaster of Bellefontaine. As a result, Kin Hubbard soon began his first regular job. His father hired him to serve as a clerk at the general delivery window in the post office. Kin was glad to get the work, although the job turned out to be a curse as well as a blessing, as he afterwards maintained.

Kin's parents were pleased that the father's gift of engraver's tools seemed to point Kin toward an involvement in journalism that suited his interests and talents. And some time after the Blaine-Logan caricatures of 1884 had been published, Kin's mother finally persuaded Kin to enroll in the Jefferson School of Art in Detroit. He stayed only a few days at the school. Certainly he did not overestimate his self-taught skill as a graphic artist when he decided that he was really far beyond the level of competence expected of a beginning art student. Kin's swift departure from the art school abruptly ended his formal training as an artist. He clearly was to be self-taught all the way, as both artist and writer. Abe Martin once said:

Experience is a dear teacher but he delivers th' goods.

Although Kin left the art school, he did not immediately leave Detroit. He lingered on for some months to sample the theatrical fare in Detroit. At this time, in dress and manner Kin quite convincingly played the role of offstage actor—or so one gathers from what he recalled: "Perhaps I should mention that at this time I was wearing a loud, plaid, cape overcoat; a close-reefed brown derby; long, narrow shoes; a massive buckthorn cane; and long matty hair. If I had been ten years older I would readily have passed for an actor of rare ability."[4]

After Kin returned from his journey to Detroit, he regularly was at work at the general delivery window in the Bellefontaine post office. But the work was tedious for a person with Kin's temperament and charged-up energy, and he did not intend to take up clerking as a permanent occupation. He worked off and on at the post office, he said, perhaps more frequently off than on. When he broke away from work at the post office, he often abruptly left Bellefontaine on foot, and alone, off on a sort of vagabond trip to some vague destination.

Kin Hubbard was always willing and eager to work at something. He needed to keep busy. Yet he was often restless and impatient, and definitely repelled by routine work. He frequently wanted to be by himself; sometimes he strongly desired to get out of town, to be stimulated by a change in environment, to make his way with strangers. Thus, in his teen-age years and beyond, Kin tried to discover himself. He tested himself in many ways as he sought his own identity. And he learned something that Abe Martin later talked about: "You can't git away from yourself by walkin' out in th' country." Intermittently, on the long, long walks out of Bellefontaine, Kin did share his parents' concern about what he should eventually become.

When Kin was in his early twenties the idea of producing his own home-talent shows in the Bellefontaine Grand Opera House possessed him, and he began to work on plans for the minstrel and vaudeville shows that he produced in the 1890s.[5] Indeed, he was heavily involved in some of these shows, serving as producer, director, stage manager, script writer, and actor. Such total immersion in theatrical activities was a joyous and enlightening experience for Kin. Especially meaningful was his creative contributions to the scripts, the earliest examples of his comic writing. For the *Grand Operatic Minstrels*, among many other things he wrote and performed a monologue listed in the program as "Kin Hubbard, Character Impersonator, Introducing His Original Misfits." These "misfits" portrayed by Kin likely were prototypes for the small-town misfit characters that Kin many years later created as citizens of Brown County, Indiana. And for the final vaudeville show that he produced, *Frank K. Hubbard's High Class Vaudevilles*, Kin wrote "funny stories," "gags," an "original society satire," and as the final act, "The Rube Circus." In this last comic piece Kin and his friend Bob Cook, later mayor of Bellefontaine, presented their interpretation of the rube clowns of the circus. Thus many years before Kin Hubbard created Abe Martin he was fond of rube characters, especially rube clowns. From all these initial forays as comic writer and performer, Kin gained valuable insight and knowledge about what makes people laugh, and he had a chance to experiment with writing comedy and portraying comic characters.

In 1891, with the help of a good friend who was delighted and impressed with the lively and very funny thumbnail sketches that Kin usually included in his letters, Kin was offered a job as staff artist at the *Indianapolis News* at a salary of twelve dollars a week. Kin took the job, but was apprehensive about being able to do the work required in the position and doubtful that he deserved the title of "artist." He later said: "I was always handicapped by not knowing how to draw. I could execute rude, sketchy caricatures that were readily recognized, but I knew nothing of composition, light and shade, and perspective."

In spite of such demurs, as Kin worked for three years at the *News* as a reporter–sketch artist he demonstrated that on his own he had acquired considerable skill in drawing. His marked ability in eye-hand coordination, his keen observation and acute visual sense, and his quick and tenacious memory all served him well in his work. Yet all the time that Kin worked so well and so industriously in Indianapolis, he really was much more interested in theatre than in art. He recalled: "I never missed a hall show or a circus, and art was farthest from my thoughts."

After an honest disagreement with a new managing editor at the *Indianapolis News* about particulars of some extremely difficult work assigned to him, Kin left the job. He then drifted through several years seemingly with little ambition and no particular incentives. He was indecisive about how he should marshal his thoughts and energy, or into what occupation, if any, he should settle. But luckily he did find work with several Ohio newspapers and thus continued to develop the skills he had begun to use so well at the *News*. In 1896 the *Tribune* of Cincinnati, Ohio, hired him for several months as a reporter–sketch artist, and later he worked several months for the Mansfield, Ohio, *News*, this time as a sketch artist and illustrator.

At long last, in 1899, and ironically right after the very successful production of *Frank K. Hubbard's High Class Vaudevilles*, Kin attentively listened to mutterings in the family about the need for him to take on some kind of regular and permanent work. By now Kin too thought that he should definitely settle on something as a permanent occupation. He decided to make a big drive for work of some kind on a newspaper. But before he began to send out inquiries he received a letter from the *Indianapolis Sun* offering him a job at fifteen dollars a week. Kin gladly accepted the offer, packed up, and left Bellefontaine—this time for good. He was thirty-one.

Kin Hubbard would not then have known that this was a turning point in his life, although he had decided to settle into something that he hoped would permanently satisfy his interests and challenge his abilities. During the first thirty years of his life he had accumulated a complex of experiences that in many ways shaped his character and directed his interests and talent toward the world of humor. But the pattern of his maturation as a person in those first three decades was random and marked by contradictions. He was curious about many things, energetic and enthusiastic, imaginative, witty, and fun-loving, restless and venturesome. And certainly when Kin was caught up and truly interested in some objective for his work or play, he strove mightily, with admirable patience and intense concentration. But in retrospect the motivation for much of his activity in those first three decades seems weak and indecisive. The most powerful and persistent interest in the years between thirteen and thirty, and the one that kept tugging Kin away from planning or preparing for a possible career in journalism, was his love affair with the theatre, a fascination that compelled him to involve himself fully in the production of minstrel and vaudeville shows.

Many years after he left Bellefontaine, Kin reviewed his life there and candidly said: "Though I didn't realize it then father's becoming postmaster was almost my undoing. At any rate it was a big handicap in life. I knew during those formative years that I could always return home, walk up to the desk behind the general delivery window and go to work at a living wage at the post office. I also had in the back of my head always the idea 'oh, well, if this job doesn't turn out, well I can go to work on the *Bellefontaine Examiner*.' It wasn't that I was lazy.

God knows I was always working at something, but I lacked incentive.
. . . While I worked hard, I dilly-dallied. I wasn't headed anywhere; I
was merely marking time. I paid a big price for the knowledge that
I had a soft place to alight, back home."[6]

Kin Hubbard thus suggests that he thoughtlessly frittered away his
life while he lived in Bellefontaine. Much from all those years was
somehow lost, he implies, because he did not early decide what he
should become. But little was really lost. Actually, much that Kin
Hubbard learned during his life at home essentially determined his
later comic perspective, his intentions, his philosophical stance as a
humorist. Indeed, a great deal of the substance of his work, and hence
his achievement as a humorist, stems directly or indirectly from his
life in Bellefontaine, Ohio. Most significantly, from thirty years of living in Bellefontaine, Kin Hubbard acquired a keen understanding and
a strong liking for what life might be like in the small towns of
America.

The Making of a Caricaturist

When Kin Hubbard left Bellefontaine perhaps fundamentally he was
better prepared than he could have imagined to succeed in the newspaper work he was to undertake in Indianapolis. At the *Indianapolis
Sun* he worked very hard as a sketch artist and caricaturist. His work
did improve. "I really made more progress as an artist during my two
years on the *Sun* than I had in all the years before." And his success
at the *Sun* paid off. In the fall of 1901, once more he was offered a job
by the *Indianapolis News* and he accepted. This time he stayed with
the *News* until the end of his career as a newspaper humorist.

At the *Sun* Kin had begun to build a good reputation for his skill in
comic drawings, and so the *News* engaged him to do small comics and
caricatures. During his long stay at the *News* Kin was to perform
many different chores, but in the three years that preceded his inven-
tion of Abe Martin, he chiefly did political caricatures. He regularly
went to the opening session of the Indiana State Legislature to make
caricatures of the new crop of legislators, the lobbyists, and the staff
people. He once said that he preferred to work on politicians with
beards and full heads of hair; doing a bald-headed legislator was "like
drawing a coconut." By this time in his experience as an artist, Kin
was swift and sure in knowing how to move from a likeness to a
caricature in his drawings. His satire of a state legislator, for example,
usually was gentle. And these caricatures were so well received and
popular that the first book he published was a collection entitled *Caricatures of Indiana State Legislators*.

MEMBERS OF THE GENERAL ASSEMBLY 1903

Courtesy of Lilly Library, Indiana
University, Bloomington, Indiana.

As part of his work as a caricaturist at the *News*—and in keeping with his own earnest and sincere interest in politics, an interest early and ardently encouraged by his father—Kin also went to local and state political conventions, and always on presidential election years he attended both the Democratic and the Republican national conventions. Over the years, in the state legislature, at the state and national conventions, and on political campaign trails Kin saw much and listened to much that gave him keen insight into the ways and means of politicians. He listened to hundreds of speeches of all kinds and in diverse situations, and of course he dipped into such experiences for the substance of his satiric comments. Politics and politicians frequently take their lumps in Abe's sayings:

It's a purty safe bet that big business donates t' a political party fer th' same lofty reason that a saloon keeper donates t' a 4th o' July celebration.

We'd all like t' vote fer th' best man, but he's never a candidate.

Th' katydids will soon be gone, but th' Indianny Legislature will meet before a great while.

Now an' then an innocent man is sent t' th' legislature.

Politicians an' actors never quit in time.

Kin had much fun and did some of his best caricatures of politicians and his best comic sketches of political events when he went on the campaign trail with candidates for state or national office. Kin once recalled politicking in Indiana: "No one but a Hoosier knows what a Presidential campaign in Indiana is like. At every stop those special trains made, throngs of excited people, brass bands, glee clubs, torch light brigades, mounted farmers, gayly bedecked maidens, grizzled wheel-horses, and women with young, greeted the statesmen and clogged the right of way."

On such a campaign trip, at the close of each day Kin mailed to the *News* his drawings of locales and incidents and the politicians and voters involved in the political activities of the day. His "news report" consisted of caricatures, cartoons, or comic strips, sometimes accompanied by descriptive passages and snips of dialogue. And frequently Kin depicted a bewhiskered country fellow in a hotel lobby at a political convention, or on the fringe of a crowd at some stop on the campaign trail in Indiana, who sometimes made a "breezy or humorous" comment, as Kin described it. These "breezy" remarks by this rustic character probably mark the dawning in Kin Hubbard's imagination of

"Abe Martin Says." And in the fall of 1904, when Kin was reporting the Roosevelt-Parker presidential campaign, he mentions that in the drawings he mailed back to the *News* he repeatedly portrayed a country character that he "rather liked."

Enter Abe Martin

Kin went on another political campaign in Indiana in the fall of 1904 that he doesn't mention in any accounts of his career. But what happened one day in that particular campaign is significant in the life and career of Abe Martin. In the fall of 1904, Kin went with John W. Kern, the Democratic nominee for Governor of Indiana, for a swing through southern Indiana. From Nashville, in Brown County, under date of October 1, 1904, Kin sent to the *News* his pictorial report about the setting for Kern's speech. Kin's drawing also vividly depicted the folks who came to hear Kern, and reflected certain aspects of life in Brown County.

On that brief visit to the tiny village of Nashville, Kin observed many things about the town and the surrounding country that later suggested to him that Brown County was where Abe Martin belonged. And the "agriculturist" he drew on that day in October 1904 certainly possessed details of dress and manner that suggest the way Kin's imagination was at work in December 1904, when he created Abe Martin.

Late that fall Kin had gone to the managing editor of the *News* and told him that he had in his sketch book many unused drawings from the fall political hustings that he hoped he could now redo and use in some way. Especially, he suggested, he had some drawings of a country fellow that he rather liked, and

CAMPAIGNING WITH KERN

he thought he might work up something with that character. The managing editor said to go ahead, so Kin got out his drawing board, sharpened his wits, and went to work. He experimented for a while with various figures, names, and locales. But his mind kept coming back to a comic character who might be something like his drawing of the "agriculturist" with the beard and huge boots down there in the hills of Brown County. On December 17, 1904, Kin put things together.

ABE MARTIN,
DECEMBER 17, 1904

The character that appeared that day established the way Abe Martin looked and spoke on the back page of the *News* for many years, except that soon Kin decided to write, daily, two unrelated sayings, instead of one sentence, under each fresh drawing of Abe. And on February 4, 1905, he gave his rustic philosopher a new and fitting environment by sending him down to the rugged hills of Brown County in southern Indiana.

ABE LEAVES FOR BROWN COUNTY

Although on one of Abe's first days traveling by foot in Brown County he is shown passing a road sign that points toward Nashville, Indiana, while close by is another sign that reads "Martin's Farm," Kin later had Abe Martin dig in for keeps on hilly, boulder-strewn farmland in Brown County, but close to the fictitious small town of Bloom Center.

ABE IN BROWN COUNTY

Soon Abe began to mention or quote other citizens of Brown County who expressed ideas in their own peculiar ways. Thus Kin Hubbard gradually created a fascinating cluster of small-town people who furnished a variety of perspectives and voices for his satiric comments. "Very often I had things to say that Abe Martin would not be likely to say, so from time to time I quoted various neighbors of his, . . . familiar country characters."

To represent the professional people of Bloom Center, one might select the redoubtable judge, Squire Marsh Swallow; genial Dr. Mopps; the schoolteacher and would-be scholar and playwright, Professor Alexander Tansey; and the ever-dynamic owner and publisher of the *Bloom Center Weekly Sliphorn*, Hon. Ex-Editor Cale Fluhart. Business enterprise in Bloom Center might be represented by Gabe Craw, bustling owner of the Little Gem Restaurant; Tell Binkley, hustling agent for tornado insurance; and Mame Moon, brawny proprietor of the local Star Livery Stable and the O.K. Used Car Lot. Miss Fawn

Lippincut, spinster, would serve as an overly ambitious literary light and inexhaustible club woman. Miss Tawney Apple supposedly fits into the scheme as a typical unsophisticated small-town girl longing for impossible big-city high romance, and Miss Germ Williams is the typical. plain girl who would settle for almost any kind of male to avoid spinsterhood. As still another part of the scheme of characterization, Constable Newt Plum, along with Squire Marsh Swallow and Judge Pusey, represents law and order. And to help identify Bloom Center as an agricultural town, over the years two farm families, Mr. and Mrs. Tilford Moots and Mr. and Mrs. Tipton Bud, and the offspring of these two couples, appear prominently in both the sayings and the Short Furrows. Conventional morality is under the watchful and firm guidance of Rev. Wiley Tanger. The viewpoint and interests of the older generation are stoutly defended by old-timers Ez Pash and Uncle Niles Turner, while the attitudes and values of the younger generation are demonstrated in the actions of bright, pretty, and flirtatious Miss Tawney Apple and the sporting young couple Mr. and Mrs. Lafe Bud.

Kin Hubbard thus peopled town and country with a captivating cast of characters. And Bloom Center and Brown County became Kin's relatively simple and stable microcosm from which Abe Martin could observe and comment on the more complex and mutable larger world outside Brown County and Indiana.

Less than a year after Kin invented Abe Martin, and at a time when he thought that the brightest promise for his future life and work seemed to lie in Indianapolis at the *News*, he decided to get married. On October 12, 1905, Frank McKinney Hubbard married Josephine Jackson. Kin declared that getting married was the best decision of his life; his greatest happiness began at that moment. The marriage to Josephine indeed did stabilize his life, and the responsibilities of married life provided a stern incentive for his work as a humorist.

The feller that puts off marryin' till he kin support a wife hain't much in love.

When son Thomas was born in 1907, and daughter Virginia in 1909, Kin was elated. His family became central in his love and interests. And from his direct experience with diverse aspects of married life he invented many of Abe's sayings. For example, as Kin's family grew up, Abe talked a lot about bringing up kids. Indeed, the psychological complexities of marriage and the intricate and sensitive interrelationships in family living became very prominent among Kin's concerns as a humorist.

Lots o' fellers git credit fer bein' self-made when they merely used ther wives' judgment.

Married life hain't so bad after you git so you kin eat the things your wife likes.

A feller never knows what he would o' done till he's been married a couple o' years.

Every father expects his boys t' do all th' things he wouldn' do when he wuz young.

Children never appreciate ther mother till they grow up an' git ont' ther father.

A son never repays his mother, but she never seems t' hold it against him.

Seven years after Kin Hubbard began to write Abe Martin's daily satiric sallies, he started to compose a brief comic essay for a feature he called "Short Furrows" that was published in each Saturday edition of the *News*. Hubbard's satiric intent and tone, as well as the subjects that he wrote about in the Short Furrows, sometimes markedly changed from week to week. Thus, in the thousand or so essays of 300 to 500 words that Kin wrote over the years, he considered from a variety of comic perspectives a comprehensive range of subjects. Abe Martin, rather than Kin Hubbard, got the by-line for the Short Furrows when they were first published in the *News*. But in many of the essays Abe's neighbors did most of the talking, and frequently the affairs of Brown County were featured. When syndicated, each essay was given a title. And whenever an essay was republished in an annual book, often a neighbor, rather than Abe, was given the by-line.

For each of the Short Furrows Kin Hubbard executed a two-column illustration. Unlike his drawings for the daily Abe Martin feature, which bore no particular relationship to the unrelated sentences placed below them, an illustration for a Short Furrow was carefully related to the central ideas of the essay. Thus when Kin was on target the illustrations significantly enhanced the satiric meaning of the Short Furrows and boosted laughter. These hundreds of pen-and-ink illustrations that tumbled from Kin Hubbard's imagination must be counted as another aspect of his talent as graphic artist turned humorist.

An event in 1910 marked a critical turning point in Kin Hubbard's life and in his career as a humorist. For the May 1910 issue of *American Magazine* Kin's friend and mentor, the well-known Hoosier humorist George Ade, wrote a brief article about Kin entitled "Abe

Martin of Brown County." In his article Ade favorably compared Kin Hubbard's creation of Abe Martin and Abe's sayings with the work of significant American humorists of the nineteenth century. And he suggested what he believed to be Kin's intent and philosophical stance as a humorist when he said that Kin had proved to be an "analytical philosopher and a good deal of a cut-up." George Ade also whetted readers' appetites for a taste of Abe Martin's horse sense and nonsense and then presented a liberal collection of Abe Martin's sayings, including:

Nobuddy kin talk as interestin' as th' feller that's not hampered by facts er information.

Nothin' a little man says ever sounds probable.

Uncle Ez Pash says his new hired man is so ding-gasted lazy thet he hed t' sharpen all th' stumps on th' farm t' keep him from settin' down.

After a feller distinguishes himself these days he starts right in t' make it pay.

As George Ade had predicted, soon after his May 1910 article appeared Kin received offers from a number of newspaper syndicates. He signed on with the George Matthews Adams Syndicate. And soon after the Short Furrows began to appear in 1911, they too were syndicated.

From the start Kin enjoyed doing the drawings for both of his features. His imagination easily conjured up images and by the time he began with Abe Martin he could draw facilely and skillfully. Writing the sayings was quite another thing—often it was a difficult and exasperating chore. A friend of Kin's at the *News* once said that part of the difficulty was caused by Kin's constant struggle to decide how "philosophical" each of Abe's sayings should be. From the beginning Kin was deeply concerned about the proportionate amount of horse sense to nonsense in his writing. He constantly had to ask himself: "What can Abe Martin possibly say next to fetch a laugh?" Should Kin first of all try to kindle the "pure, genuine laughter" that he had one of his characters, Professor Gayno Hawk, so eloquently describe? Or should serious intent most often inform Abe's sayings so that readers might think and feel first, and then laugh?

In the light of what we know about Kin Hubbard's experience with life up to the time he created Abe Martin, it seems natural that in the early years Abe chiefly talked about subjects that people in small towns could understand, things they liked to think about and might laugh at. And so it was. Early on, Abe's sayings had much to do with small-town affairs, with life in a country village. And in the early almanacs, especially, Abe talked a lot about country folks and life on a farm. Thus, before Abe Martin Says and the Short Furrows were first syndicated, Kin Hubbard seems to favor Abe Martin as clown, and tilts his humor toward nonsense and "pure, genuine laughter."

With syndication Kin acquired a horde of readers across the nation. As a composite audience they represented a great diversity of attitudes and interests and beliefs. Kin realized that to capture and satisfy the interest of such a mixture of readers, Abe had to talk often about the political or social ideas or issues with which a majority of his fellow countrymen were currently concerned. But not everything Abe said could be about current matters. To perk the interest of his older readers, for instance, Abe often nostalgically hearkened back to earlier times. Increasingly, however, Kin had Abe talking about current things that almost everyone was thinking about. After syndication, then, and especially in the 1920s, Kin seems to favor Abe Martin as philosopher and in his humor inclined more and more to "horse sense" and "thoughtful laughter."

Abe Martin, Cracker-Barrel Philosopher and Clown

Over the years, in fascinating ways, Kin Hubbard worked out Abe's dual function as philosopher and clown. To make Abe believable in his role as clown, Kin first of all made him clownlike in his physical appearance and dress. Other comic elements are also evident in Abe Martin's antic actions and in the environment in which he roamed. Such details helped readers accept as appropriate and believable Abe's tall tales, his nonsense sayings, and the extravagant humor of some of the Short Furrows.

With equal care, but in a different way, Kin Hubbard prepared Abe Martin to play his role as philosopher. As Kin developed the horse-sense part of Abe's character, he seemed to carry in his imagination the image of a cracker-barrel philosopher, a prominent and very popular comic figure in nineteenth- and early twentieth-century American literature and journalism.

The model cracker-barrel philosopher is a country person in a small agricultural town in nineteenth-century America. He is a small-town citizen, well-known locally as a sharp, witty, independent sort of fellow, and he can be frequently found holding forth in the general store. He has little formal education but a lot of common sense. ("Ther' hain't

Speakin' o' big crowds, we recall when Bryan spoke here, jest before his last defeat, a woman passed her baby o'er th' heads o' th' crowd fer th' Commoner t' kiss, an' when she got her kid back he wuz married an' settled in Kokomo.

nothin' as uncommon as common sense.") As this confident rustic "philosophizes" about a great variety of matters, he nonchalantly confiscates pieces of cheese from the handy store-cheese on the counter. This he nibbles at, along with soda crackers that he deftly lifts from a nearby cracker barrel—the barrel on which he sometimes sits. And there you have it: a cracker-barrel philosopher.

The cracker-barrel philosopher can be identified in other ways. He sometimes appears to be "just folks." As such, he seems to represent a mass of Americans who are somewhere in the middle between extremes in wealth or poverty, or extremes in education, or extremes in attitudes, or interests, or beliefs. The cracker-barrel philosopher also sometimes adroitly plays the role of "wise fool." And what he says—most often in a rural dialect—frequently includes homely metaphors, or popular maxims, or paradoxical epigrams.[7]

Abe Martin says:

If th' meek ever do inherit th' earth some one'll git it away from 'em before they have it an hour.

Some folks git credit fer havin' hoss sense that haint ever had money enough t' make fools o' 'emselves.

A friend is like a umbreller. He's never there when you want him, an' if he is he's broke.

Money talks an' that's th' reason why so many o' us git drowned out o' th' conversation.

Th' feller that agrees with ever'thing you say is either a fool er he is gittin' ready t' skin you.

Th' safest way t' double your money is t' fold it over once an' put it back in your pocket.

Significantly, Abe Martin's habitat seems to certify that he comments on affairs of the larger world from the perspective of a small-town citizen. His ethical judgments are based on values, attitudes, and moral codes presumably valid and viable in small towns throughout America. Thus Kin Hubbard sought to develop in Abe the philosopher-like qualities that make his commonsensical comments believable.

But over the years, as Kin Hubbard developed Abe Martin as a cracker-barrel philosopher and as his primary spokesman, he made very interesting changes in Abe's outer appearance and in his character. From February 1905 until about 1920, Abe remained pretty much the way he appeared on the cover of Kin Hubbard's first annual book.

But about ten years after syndication started, Abe began to come from Kin's drawing board somewhat changed from his early image. The slouch is less evident; the whiskers have dropped down; Abe wears a different hat that rides at a rakish angle. He is still essentially clown-like in appearance, but he is now spruced-up in dress, looks younger, more alert and sprightly. Overall, perhaps Abe looks less like a shrewd country bumpkin, more like an impish, witty-wise small-town citizen. For the most part, probably the latter-day Abe Martin more believably communicates Kin Hubbard's satiric observations of American society in the 1920s.

EARLY ABE

Abe Martin's Sayings

The popularity of Abe Martin, both as philosopher and as clown, was due chiefly to those two unrelated sentences that Kin daily for twenty-six years placed under a fresh drawing of Abe on the back page of the *Indianapolis News.* Kin referred to the sentences he wrote for Abe Martin in various ways: "Comments of Abe Martin," "Abe Martin's sayings," "Abe Martin's wisecracks." In other instances he called them epigrams or "epigrammatic sayings." The combination of two unrelated sentences was a "paragraph." The sentences most often are

LATER ABE

called sayings, and one common definition of the word "saying" is something said that is like a maxim or an adage. Many of Abe Martin's comments are indeed very like maxims. But Kin Hubbard also constructed sentences for Abe in other ways. Sometimes his comment resembles an anecdote:

Prof. Alex Tansey, our school teacher, wuz discussin' th' weighin' o' th' human soul. He says it reminds him of a' episode in his home town, Angoly, when a party o' local scientists tried t' weigh a bunghole by first weighin' th' barrel.

And here is a one-sentence anecdote:

Pinky Kerr asked Tell Binkley how many soldiers Napoleon had at Austerlitz, an' he said: "I don't know; I haint seen a newspaper fer a month."

Frequently Kin constructed sentences that contained sensory imagery and were cast in the form of similes or metaphors:

Th' worst drawback t' hot weather is th' odor that hovers about some folks like they wuz runnin' with th' emergency brakes on.

When Franklin P. Adams said that he liked Kin Hubbard as a humorist because he could get a whole novel into a sentence, Adams probably had in mind a sentence such as the following:

This mornin' Tell Binkley jumped int' his new three-thousand-dollar tourin' car, an', after testing th' carburator, hurried t' th' poor farm, arrivin' jist ten minutes too late t' see his mother alive.

Perhaps the most compelling and popular sentences that Kin wrote were those that he called epigrams or epigrammatic sayings. Such sentences usually possess the salient characteristics of epigrams: they are witty, ingenious, pointed, and tersely expressed. Furthermore, they often have a particular element recommended in this recipe for making an epigram.

The qualities rare in a bee that we meet
  In an epigram never should fail;
The body should always be little and sweet
  And a sting should be left in the tail.

And here is a handful of sayings that demonstrate how effectively Kin could place a "sting" in the tail!

A woman's work is never done—anymore.

People that can't sing never refuse.

Miss Fawn Lippincut sings with feelin', but not fer others.

We hain't given near enough thought to th' other simple things o' life, besides women.

Best of all, perhaps, Kin sometimes produced his own original versions of familiar adages. For example, take the old saying "All that glitters is not gold," and listen to Abe Martin:

Th' first thing t' turn green in th' Spring is th' Christmas jewelry.

And some sayings seem to be parodies of maxims:

He who hesitates is saved.

If everybuddy thought before they spoke ther' wouldn' be enough noise in this world t' scare a jay bird.

Kin Hubbard wrote thousands of witty, terse, and pointed sentences on many different subjects. But his comic intent, and hence the kind of laughter he hoped to arouse, might vary greatly from sentence to sentence. Take, for example, the varying satiric force with which he treated the problem of "bringing up the kids." Kin could write two moderately satiric sentences like these:

We never know how a boy is goin' t' turn out, or when a girl is goin' to' turn in.

Th' trouble is most parents don't worry about a daughter till she fails t' show up fer breakfast, and then it's too late.

Then he wrote this devastating sentence:

"Well, we know where she is now," said Mrs. Em Moots, t'day, when her daughter wuz buried.

Kin Hubbard's sentences, constructed in various ways to achieve various ends, probably constitute the weightiest and most significant part of his achievements as a humorist. And first place among the epigrammatic sayings that should enjoy a long life must go to those that expose to laughter the common foibles and quirks and imperfections of all of us. These wise, well-reasoned sayings reveal Kin Hubbard's sound judgments about motives for human action. They do indeed seem to express a truth based on common sense and the practical experience of mankind.

Nobuddy ever forgets where he buried a hatchet.

Th' hardest kind o' prosperity t' stand is a neighbor's.

It's what we learn after we think we know it all that counts.

Flattery won't hurt you if you don't swallow it.

William McDermot said that Kin was the "greatest maker of epigrams in America." If that is a judicious statement, then it is high praise indeed, because there have been many accomplished makers of maximlike satiric sentences in this country. Some American humorists who wrote epigrammatic sayings for their characters no doubt influenced the work of Kin Hubbard, including Kin's contemporary Finley Peter Dunne, with his cracker-barrel philosopher "Mr. Martin Dooley." But by the 1920s, when Abe Martin was coming on strong, Mr. Dooley was silent. It can be claimed, then, that Abe Martin was the last of the significant comic characters in the tradition of the nineteenth-century cracker-barrel philosopher. And we can confidently say that Kin Hubbard was one of the most prolific and accomplished makers of epigrams that the country has ever known. This part of Kin's work constitutes a significant contribution to our heritage of humor in America.

The Annual Books: Abe Martin for Christmas

In 1906, just about a year after he married Josephine Jackson, Kin decided to capitalize on the increasing popularity of his comic spokesman Abe Martin by publishing a book of Abe's collected sayings. And so in the fall of 1906, to catch the Christmas trade, Kin brought out his first little book, *Abe Martin of Brown County, Indiana*. The book consisted chiefly of a series of paragraphs, each of which contained two unrelated sentences—the "sayings"—as they had first appeared in the *News*.

What this country needs is a big, lively back t' th' farm movement, startin' at Washington. Ther's jist one chance fer an ugly girl— amiability.

In *Abe Martin* there was also a section labeled "Abe Martin: His Neighbors." For this feature of his book Kin Hubbard made original drawings of some of the characters who later became Abe's neighbors in Brown County. And for each such personage Kin wrote a brief, comic, tongue-in-cheek biography, chiefly intended to delight readers and make them laugh, rather than to inform them by presenting character-defining biographical details. This first book also had an introduction by Kin Hubbard's novelist friend Meredith Nicholson, who said that Abe Martin was "Plato on a cracker barrel" and that Abe's neighbors were "veritable figures snatched boldly from the rural landscape." Another Hoosier friend of Kin's, the popular poet James Whitcomb Riley, wrote a little poem for the book that he called "Riley's Tribute." Riley dedicated the poem to "Kin Hubbard, the Father of His Countryman, Abe Martin." It began with these lines:

ABE MARTIN!—dad-burn his old picture!
P'tends he's a Brown County fixture—
A kind of comical mixture
    Of hoss-sense and no sense at all! . . .

The first edition of *Abe Martin* rapidly sold out, and before Christmas of 1906 two other printings were rushed to market. Kin Hubbard, surprised and delighted by the resounding success of this first book, decided then and there that in November of each year, to meet the Christmas trade, he would bring out other books. Most of the twenty-four annual books that followed chiefly contained a combination of comic essays and Abe Martin sayings. Several of the books, however, also carried additional drawings of neighbors, with accompanying comic biographies. And in some years Kin Hubbard departed from such patterns. For 1907, and for four other years—1908, 1909, 1911, 1921—the annual book professed to be an "Almanack." Kin Hubbard's almanacks usually contained many of Abe Martin's epigrammatic sayings and a few comic essays allegedly written by Abe's "neighbors." But in the almanacks Kin Hubbard intended chiefly to parody materials similar to those that might have been found in Ben Franklin's seventeenth-century *Poor Richard's Almanack*, or in the *Old Farmer's Almanack*. When Kin's first *Almanack* came out, however, it was suggested that he also had modeled his book on—or perhaps had even received inspiration for writing it from—the work of the American humorist Henry W. Shaw, who wrote a burlesque *Josh Billings' Old Farmer's Allminax* (1870–79). Possibly Kin had in mind all of these sources. Anyway, he slyly implied his satiric intentions when he introduced his first almanack by saying that it would contain:

> Timely hints to farmers and young women,
> actual facts about the moon, astrological
> lore, true explanation of dreams, famous
> political speeches, rare philosophical
> musings. . .

Occasionally over the years, in addition to the almanacks and the books exclusively containing collections of sayings and comic essays, Kin Hubbard published other kinds of comic productions, such as *Velma's Vow* (1916) and *The Lost Heiress of Red Stone Hall* (1910), novels professedly written by Miss Fawn Lippincut. These two pieces were burlesques of the sentimental and melodramatic novels of the time.

Publishing the annual books was a joyful and lucrative part of Kin Hubbard's activities as a humorist. And presumably each year he selected for publication what currently were his most effective and compelling comic productions. Thus Kin Hubbard's selected work, attractively displayed in the twenty-five annual volumes, presents a comprehensive and engaging overview of his comic world.

A review of Kin Hubbard's activities at the *Indianapolis News* from 1901 to his death in 1930 reveals the surprising range and volume of his productivity as a humorist. He started out on the art staff at the *News*, chiefly doing caricatures of state and national politicians, and continued with such work throughout his career. In December of 1904 he began the Abe Martin feature and for twenty-six years met an inexorable deadline of 9:00 A.M. for his daily fresh drawing of Abe and two unrelated satiric sentences. The yield from such efforts: about eight thousand drawings and sixteen thousand sayings. In October of 1911, Kin began to write the weekly comic essays, Short Furrows, published in the Saturday edition of the *News* under the by-line of Abe Martin. He wrote about a thousand Short Furrows. Abe Martin and his sayings were syndicated in 1910, and syndication of the Short Furrows soon followed. Thereafter, Abe Martin merrily traveled throughout the country, gradually attracting a host of devotees. In November of 1906, Kin began to publish the annual books. Usually he managed all details of composition for each book, engaged a local printer, and listed as publishers the Abe Martin Publishing Co. The annual books chiefly contained selected sayings and Short Furrows previously published in the *News*. But Kin worked up much fresh and special comic material for some books and usually executed original illustrations. The characters who became Abe's neighbors were chiefly developed in the annual books. Kin relished getting out these books, and the twenty-five slim volumes that he published contain much of his best work as a humorist. He always signed on as author of the annual books; for all else he remained anonymous, letting Abe Martin or Abe's neighbors do the talking.

Kin Hubbard accomplished a prodigious amount of good work in his sixty-two years. And he worked and lived intensely, retaining a youthful spirit and his full powers as a humorist until the very end.

In the early morning of December 26, 1930, Kin Hubbard suffered a sudden heart attack. In a few minutes he was gone. To a multitude of Americans who knew his work, Kin Hubbard's death indeed seemed a national tragedy. And the cold realization that Abe Martin and Abe's neighbors would speak no more was central to the sense of loss expressed. No longer would millions of Americans turn the pages in hundreds of newspapers all over the country to see what Abe Martin had to say that day.

But there is no need for sorrow now. Let laughter reign. Abe Martin is back again! As you explore the abundant harvest of Kin Hubbard's laughter presented here, you will meet Abe Martin in both the sayings and the Short Furrows, and you will get acquainted with some of Abe's neighbors. And that's not all. You are going to come across a sheaf of select pieces and—oh happy find!—a sampler Abe Martin's Almanack. Hurry on, now. Abe Martin is waiting for you!

NOTES

1. George Ade, "Abe Martin of Brown County," *American Magazine*, May 1910, p. 46.
2. Frank McKinney Hubbard, *Indianapolis News*, LXIII, No. 17, December 26, 1930. p. 1. Unless otherwise indicated, the self-descriptive quotations attributed to Kin Hubbard in this introductory chapter are taken from the autobiographical sketches which appeared in the *News* on December 26, 1930, the day of Kin Hubbard's death.
3. Fred C. Kelly, " 'Kin' Hubbard Has Won Fame by Writing Two Sentences a Day," *American Magazine*, April 1924, p. 190.
4. Fred C. Kelly, *The Life and Times of Kin Hubbard Creator of Abe Martin* (New York: Farrar, Straus and Young, 1952), p. 60. Quoted by Kelly from an autobiographical sketch by Kin Hubbard.
5. Information about these productions is derived from theatre programs and flyers in possession of Thomas Hubbard, Bellefontaine, Ohio.
6. Kelly, *Life and Times of Kin Hubbard*, pp. 61–62.
7. Norris W. Yates, "The Crackerbox Oracle," *The American Humorist* (Ames, Iowa: Iowa State University Press, 1964), pp. 21–22.

PART TWO

The Harvest
of Laughter

"... But, my friends, we shouldn'
care what laughter is or what causes
it, but we should rejoice in th' fact
that we are able t' laugh, not grin or
titter, but laugh loud an' hearty, bois-
terous if you please, fer ther is no
exercise in th' world more healthful
t' body an' soul than pure, genuine
laughter."

Professor Gayno Hawk

ABE MARTIN, PHILOSOPHER AND CLOWN

We see that Abe Martin, like his creator, avidly followed the news, ready to pounce on something he just had to talk about. In the 1920s many of Abe's sayings dealt tartly with extreme trends in manners and idiotic fads in dress. And, among many other subjects, he especially had much to say about crime, bringing up the kids, Prohibition, and the mixed blessings of rampant prosperity. But when Abe wanted to talk more at length about the aberrations of married life, he let go in one of the Short Furrows.

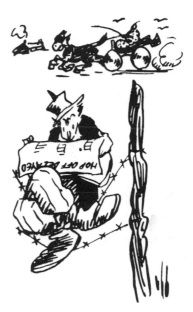

No feller ever ort t' publish a book unless he's got a trade t' fall back on. Seems like th' folks that have th' least use for knowledge have th' most.

Abe Martin was born at Roundhead, Hardin County, Ohio, some time between the first and second Seminole War. He got his early education in a general store and played a yellow clarinet in a band on Johnson's Island, Lake Erie, during the Rebellion of which we have all heard so much. After his outing was broken up he went to Brown County, Indiana, to reside with his wife's folks. Mr. Martin votes the Democratic ticket for nothing and is a student of the film and drama. He eats sardines between the acts and boasts of having seen "The Hidden Hand" twenty-one times and Julia Marlowe in "Pinafore" once. He says politics is just one five-cent cigar after another and that the union was preserved so ball players could practice in the South.

Miss Mame Moon has a new one piece hobble dress an' she looks like an upright walrus.

Most of the girls that come out o' beauty shops look like they hadn't been waited on.

"Goin' back t' long skirts agin would be jest like lockin' th' barn after th' hoss has been stolen," said the Rev. Wiley Tanger, t'day.

A snapshot o' th' modern girl walkin' looks like a radish.

I don't think much of a dance where th' girl looks like she wuz bein' carried out of a burnin' building.

Some girls seem t' buy a skirt on th' theory that they'll never set down.

"Ther's two kinds o' husbands I wouldn' have—th' kind that sticks his money in his business as fast as he gits it, an' th' kind that don't make none, an' I've tried 'em both," declares Mrs. Lee Swank.

Why can't ever' couple git along like Link Gage an' his wife? Ever' mornin', unless its cold or rainin', he kisses her goodby at th' bus as she goes t' work.

You can shoot husbands th' year round in some states.

Next t' worryin' about th' home life o' English sparrows, th' silliest waste o' time is concernin' ourselves with th' domestic affairs o' movie people.

Those who've seen Aimee McPherson seem rather inclined t' believe she wuz kidnapped, but they don't believe she walked back.

One o' the great industries o' th' present age is rebuildin' those who have passed middle age.

Th' Constitution follers th' flag, an' th' off color story follers th' cocktail.

You can't stop a thing by makin' a crime of it.

We hain't got prohibition. It only costs more.

"If I ever git caught I want to be tried by a senate committee," said Bootlegger Ike Soles, t'day.

Don't kick on a hangover, fer you're lucky if you even wake up.

Hardly anybuddy would work fer what ther worth.

"Who's lap wuz you on last night?" Lafe Bud asked his wife, an' she said, "I didn' git his name but he's th' husband o' that woman that you carried out t' th' car."

"Bootleggers on th' run," says a newspaper, but that's cause they're back on ther orders.

Anybuddy that ever tried t' git rid of a chew o' terbacker at an art exhibit kin appreciate how terrifyin' it must be t' try stash a torso.

This is a loose, fast age, an' at the rate we're goin' jazz'll soon run its course, an' then watch th' demand fer decent, unscuffed girls.

"I'm allus glad when my husbands git killed by autos, fer then I ain't accused o' poisonin' 'em," said Mrs. Em Painter, as she left th' cemetery.

I don't know which is passin' out th' fastest—horse sense or horses.

Peace is th' greatest o' all blessin's, but you've got t' be awful poor an' obscure t' git any.

What th' country needs is a good, tough two-dollar bill that'll last as long as it takes t' save one.

Some folks are born in society, an' some are coaxed in, but a large per cent o' them tunnel in.

Wouldn't it be fine if people were known fer what they are instead of what they belong to?

I'll say this for adversity—people seem to be able to stand it an' that's more'n I kin say fer prosperity.

When Judge Pusey asked Lon Moon, who murdered his wife, if he had anything t' say before bein' acquitted, he replied, "I never would have shot her if I'd knowed I'd have t' go through so much red tape."

SHORT FURROWS
By ABE MARTIN

For years most folks have been under th' impression that our feathered friends choose ther mates fer life, an' that inconstancy is unknown amongst birds. Nothin' could be more remote from th' truth. Fer nearly five months o' th' past summer an' fall I kept close watch on a couple o' mated blackbirds. They got on fairly well t'gether. They had some spats, an', while th' female bird wuzn' altogether what she should have been, they managed t' stick it out till fall, when th' male bird left fer Floridy with another party. I've known crows t' have three or four wives in a season, an' kingfishers are notorious Mormons, an' poor providers. I used t' know a kingfisher that et ever'thing he caught, an' his mate had t' neglect her family t' git food. Robins are th' best home makers, an' I've known young robins t' hang around ther folks till frost, an' never turn a hand toward feedin' 'emselves. Yes, robins is th' most indulgent parents of all birds. I've seen a mother robin lead a youngster right up t' a worm an' point it out, but, in spite o' all she could do, she finally had t' pick it up fer th' youngster an' hand it t' him. Young robins will not work till they jest have to. We're all given t' thinkin' th' home life o' wrens is ideal, an' we often speak o' some married acquaintances as livin' t'gether like two wrens. I've watched wrens by th' month an' ther mean, little, underhanded sneaks as a rule. O' course, ther's some highly respectable wrens, wrens you'd gladly have on your premises, but jest th' same, I know some wrens that are guilty o' all th' crimes in th' calendar. All o' that purty stuff is put on fer effect, an' once you see 'em in ther homes, or 'way off from human eyes, you'll see that they carry on somethin' terrible. I'm speakin' o' th' general run o' wrens. O'course, ther's exceptions, same as there is 'mongst turkey buzzards. Some turkey buzzards have high ideals an' are true t' ever' obligation in life, but I've watched 'em fer weeks an' weeks an' most o' them are as bad as any human bein'. Perhaps, turtle doves, or wood doves, lead lives as blameless as it's possible t' live 'em an' git by, but they have lots o' human traits, an' 'll listen t' reason if they think they kin git away with it. Th' jaybird is good t' his folks, but he's a natural thief an' murderer, an' works fast. Ther's lots o' mawkish sentiment in regard t' th' tiny peewee. Th' peewee is a vicious little bandit, an' it's only thro' fear that he refrains from attackin' us. If those o' you who are interested in nature an' love bird life 'll jest take a month off in th' fall an' snoop around an' watch th' goin' away parties among our migratory birds you'll have your eyes opened. That's th' splittin' up time when th' loves an' th' romances o' th' summer season are tossed aside an' fergotten in th' rush t' beat it fer Miammy. Most birds only stick t'gether till ther children are big enough t' hop off, so birds are purty human after all.

ABE MARTIN'S
NEIGHBORS

Now that we've briefly looked at Abe Martin in action, let's get acquainted with some of his neighbors, the typical country characters that Kin Hubbard created to express some of the things that Abe might not say. This engaging group of small-town people includes Miss Fawn Lippincut, Prof. Alexander Tansey, Tell Binkley, Uncle Niles Turner, Mame Moon, Lafe Bud, Editor Cale Fluhart, Constable Newt Plum, Dr. Mopps, Grandma Pash, Ez Pash, Mr. and Mrs. Tilford Moots, "Pinky" Kerr, Mr. and Mrs. Tipton Bud, Miss Tawney Apple, Miss Germ Williams, Squire Marsh Swallow, Rev. Wiley Tanger, Judge Pusey, Clem Harner, and Gabe Craw.

Some of Abe Martin's neighbors became well known and popular right along with Abe. If one takes hints from Kin Hubbard's pen-and-ink portraits and his brief biographical accounts of Abe Martin's neighbors, and then observes what they say and do in the sayings and in the Short Furrows, individuals begin to assume identities somewhat as in the following character sketches.

Miss Fawn Lippincut

Fawn is getting along in years—number not mentioned. She remembers most fondly the five years she was eighteen. Fawn is a panicky spinster, not yet reconciled to oldmaidhood. She's smart, energetic and ambitious and dresses neatly and properly, although she lags quite a bit in style. Fawn comes from a very dramatic family. Her mother kept a theatrical boarding house, and her father was a trap drummer who traveled with a troupe of players that produced *Uncle Tom's Cabin*—he tore paper for the snow scene. But Fawn is talented in her own right. As a mere child Fawn recited "Twinkle, Twinkle, Little Star" 500 times, always with much success. She still recites almost anything, including "Twinkle, Twinkle"—without urging. And now Fawn is also an eager songstress who composes her own songs, words and music. She has one song that has become very popular locally: "Don't Go Down Town After Supper, Father, Dear." In addition, Fawn is the locally acclaimed authoress of a novel, *Velma's Vow*, and she also writes voluminously for the *Bloom Center Weekly Sliphorn*, but concentrates on such regular weekly features as "M'Lady's Corner" and "Fawn Lippincut's Queries and Answers."

Fawn is an indefatigable club woman and organizer of local social events, as well as a feisty advocate of women's rights. And as a mildly spicy gossip, she manages to keep abreast, or maybe a little ahead, of everything that's going on in town.

Kin Hubbard carefully watched the proliferation of insipid etiquette and womanly-advice features in magazines and newspapers. When he decided to expose such stuff to ridicule, he turned to Miss Fawn Lippincut and the Bloom Center Weekly Sliphorn.

QUERIES AND ANSWERS
MISS FAWN LIPPINCUTT

How may I destroy the odour of a grocery cigar?—Ethyl.
ANSWER—By burning a trunk strap.

How may I keep a college athlete from kissing me if he wants to?—Mell.

ANSWER—Send me a self-addressed stamped envelope.

I am very thin and inclined to whine in unguarded moments, yet I have many gentlemen admirers. Is there any accounting for infatuations?—Belle.

ANSWER—No.

I am very popular but I have no evening clothes. How shall I proceed?—Bob.

ANSWER—Stick to your present system.

Is there any rule for cutting steak after it has been served to you?—Maud.

ANSWER—The recipient of a piece of steak should keep one foot on the floor while cutting it.

I am madly in love with a worthless gentleman but my mother objects to him. Are worthy young men ever attractive?—Caprice.

ANSWER—There are isolated instances.

Is wax-flower making a lost art?—Adelaide.

ANSWER—Yes, and there is no reward.

Can there be perfect happiness where the husband is absolutely sure of his wife's love?—Garnet.

ANSWER—No.

Will you please suggest some pleasant remedy for the liver besides buttermilk? I am frail and do not admire it.—Fanchette.

ANSWER—Riding on an elephant.

I am a worthy young man of splendid habits and good prospects. I have ushered at seventeen church weddings and put up thirty-two hammocks so far this season, and yet the girls do not seem to care for me.—Ersie.

ANSWER—Intersperse your exemplary habits with an occasional rash act.

Is it permissible to hold hands with a young man who has only called on me once?—Madge.

ANSWER—It is often necessary.

I have a little boy nine years old that can draw anything. Will you suggest some good art school where I may send him?—Pap.

ANSWER—You have a remarkable child. I do not know of any art school that needs him.

My husband buys forty-five cents worth of mixed drinks every time I send him for a five-cent loaf of bread. How long will we keep our home?—Margery.

ANSWER—It takes longer to drink up some homes than it does others. Try baking your own bread.

Later

Your kind suggestion was acted upon and our home will be sold under the hammer to-morrow.—Margery.

MISMATIN' AN' OTHER THINGS

MISS FAWN LIPPINCUT

My dear Miss Lippincut:

Like hundreds o' other girls at seventeen I married th' only man I thought I could ever love without lookin' around a little. I have no profession er other means o' livlihood an' it has worked a hardship on both o' us. If I wuz single agin I believe I could do better. Do you believe in second marriages?—Despondent.

What possible objection kin ther be t' second marriages? If men fail at ever'thing they undertake an' finally land a government job, why should some poor, misguided girl who has wed th' only man she could ever love at seventeen be allowed t' starve?... After two er three seasons o' shiverin' around a base burner, runnin' up bills fer malted milk an' nipples at th' corner drug store, tryin' t' raise a fern er trimmin' th' same ole hat over an' over, Love gits purty tired an' packs up a few belongin's an' ducks out. After a while Sentiment hands in her resignation an' th' average marriage then becomes a cold business proposition.

Ther's lots o' difference between th' ole perfume laden June nights on th' verandy hidden by sweet climbin' honeysuckles an' tryin' t' operate a double oven, six-cylinder cook stove with a baby on th' floor cryin' fer a warm bottle an' a husband walkin' thro' th' kitchen with his watch out....

In half civilized Thibet a woman kin have as many husbands as she pleases, t' support. In China a widow must stay single till all o' her husband's folks die, an' an American Indian squaw must remain a widow for seven years, with two off fer good behavior.

A girl takes th' same chances when she marries as a man takes when he buys a pair o' two-dollar patent leather shoes, an' she should have th' same inalienable right, when her husband breaks on th' sides, t' look around fer somethin' better. Suppose your own daughter in an unguarded moment should marry a roller skatin' professor?

Here's a personal about Fawn from the Bloom Center Weekly Sliphorn:

On Tuesday Miss Fawn Lippincut got her new sunback dress on frontwards an' had t' back all th' way to th' pustoffice an' home again.

Also, Fawn once said:

Next t' a suitcase full o' p'taters there hain't nothin' as hard t' lug around as a secret.

Professor Alexander Tansey

Professor Tansey is in his early forties (approximately). He is confident, superficially articulate, and grossly charming. Although practically uneducated, he teaches in the local schools. When asked by the school board whether the Mississippi River flows north or south, Professor Tansey quickly replied: "I teach both ways!" Tansey is a would-be intellectual, however, who likes to dabble in multiple fields of learning. Sometimes he aspires to the law. At night he also reads a little medicine. He gave the medical world a jolt by declaring that "a wig grows after death." He is an industrious amateur archeologist and an eager birdwatcher. From time to time Prof. Tansey writes articles for the magazine *Pleasant Moments*—and other big Eastern publications. But perhaps most ardently Prof. Tansey aspires to be a playwright and has just finished writing *The Slaves of Catarrh* and *The Butcher's Bride; or, The Runaway Hearse.* Much in demand as a public speaker, he will talk—at great length—on just about any subject.

When Kin Hubbard wanted to poke fun at extreme aberrations in women's dress during the 1920s, he assigned the chore to Professor Alexander Tansey and had him address a local women's organization, Th' Home Trainin' League.

TH' DECLINE O' MODESTY

PROFESSOR ALEXANDER TANSEY

"One o' th' most remarkable things t'day, at least t' my notion, is how a man in th' full possession o' his faculties can keep his mind on his business when he looks about him. I wish t' say, if I may be permitted t' do so, that th' effect o' th' slashed skirt toward retardin' moral progress in this country kin scarcely be comprehended, much less estimated.

"Those o' you whose memories kin go back t' th' Jersey waist an' th' Muncie roller skate must be appalled when you stand on th' postoffice corner any afternoon, rain er shine—rain preferred—an' note th' progress degeneracy in dress has made since those stirrin' days o' th' early eighties. If it wuz a mistake t' give independence t' Cuby how fer greater wuz th' mistake t' give independence t' th' waist line? Many problems in th' home t'day are directly traceable t' th' ever shiftin' an' migratory waist line....

"T'day our current literature is teemin' with brazen underwear advertisements an' sickly romances. A great full-page picture that probably cost eight times as much as th' story will show a limp gazelle-eyed queen wrigglin' an' smilin' in th' embrace o' a faultlessly dressed pianner mover with a jardiniere o' palms fer a background. Under th' inspirin' scene we read: 'Claspin' Imogene passionately in his strong arms Harold kissed her agin, an' agin, an' agin.' Right now many daughters in our best homes are anxiously waitin' fer th' July number t' see whether Harold married th' girl er ran away....

"Agin we are face t' face with another short sleeve summer with its burnt forearms an' goat knee elbows. Will nothin' save us from this annual ordeal we may well ask?

"In these days o' skimpy apparel an' extravagant pleasure th' serious minded girl is as scarce as fish at a fishin' resort, an' th' tango frock an' flat heels, superinduced by th' sloppy Peruvian amble, will, if I may be permitted t' express it, be a constant menace t' th' traffic along th' road t' success....

"But, my friends, th' most astonishin' thing o' all is how anything as sensible as th' shirt waist has held on all these years."

It was widely believed in Kin Hubbard's time that success in many aspects of business, but particularly in salesmanship, depended primarily on a radiant personality that could readily be cultivated. When Kin went after this sham, Professor Alexander Tansey, who might believably have subscribed to such a notion, was his spokesman.

PERSONAL MAGNETISM

PROFESSOR ALEX TANSEY

Personal magnetism is that quality in human nature which enables a feller t' git by with a red carnation in his lapel an' little ability—that indefinable somethin' which enables us t' appeal t' others with success.

Personal magnetism, like th' squash, may be cultivated an' developed.... Th' next time you see a promoter, or a politician, carefully study his magnetic quality. He may not have a warm, soggy clasp o' th' hand or a fireman's mustache, an' he may not be dressed accordin' t' th' magazine ads or belong t' any lodges. But ther's somethin' about him which attracts you t' him. You realize he's got your number an' that it's useless t' plead....

Magnetism means social as well as financial success, since it makes warm useful friends without th' aid o' money.

Th' first step in developin' personal magnetism is t' learn t' be cheerful tho' bored. A wide radiant smile is th' foundation o' magnetism. But a smile t' be effective must have a well ordered background. Th' teeth should be plugged an' evened up. After you've mastered th' art o' smilin' an' bein' cheerful begin t' train yourself t' sayin' an' doin' only agreeable things, rememberin' that one little mean act'll counteract a whole day's smile....

O' course if you're well fixed you kin do without personal magnetism. But if you're jest startin' out in life with a piano half paid fer personal magnetism is invaluable.

What a pity it is that so many o' us refuse t' become acquainted with our own great powers, but instead prefer t' struggle along an' toady after those who have seen th' light an' found th' way.

Tell Binkley

Tell Binkley is in his middle sixties. He is pompous, loud, free-wheeling, sometimes unscrupulous. He is also altogether charming—when it will get him something. Tell is Bloom Center's perpetual-motion business man, entrepreneur, and super salesman. He sells tornado insurance regularly, and specious gold-mine stock whenever he can.

As a jolly glad-hander and slick talker, Tell has crashed his way into all the local civic organizations and social clubs. At one time he was President and Treasurer of the Brown County Trust, an institution established for the savings of widows and children. But due to Tell Binkley's lavish generosity to his friends—and himself—the bank precipitously had to close its doors. In addition to conducting sundry local business enterprises, Tell automatically runs for some kind of local political office. Somebody once said that "Tell would be a much better politician if he didn't hold a baby like it was a Roman candle."

Tell is an incurable public speaker, much in demand to make prophetic pronouncements about economic conditions, in particular, and party politics of the future, in general.

Kin Hubbard once wrote up a list of statements that he ascribed to Abe Martin's businessman neighbor—Tell Binkley's "Service" Creed:

"George Washington never told a lie, but he was also a poor businessman."

"Fer ever' feller that's got a little dab o' money ther's ten fellers figurin' on how they're goin' t' separate him from it."

"All men are born equal, but some are better than others on th' getaway."

"If money didn't talk you'd never know some folks wuz around."

"Nobuddy ever got such a good salary that they didn' lie about it."

"Photos are like friends—we never have over one or two good ones in a life time."

"Some folks are jest like trained seals—you've got t' keep handin' 'em somethin'."

"Ther's lots o' honest people who never had a good chance t' be anything else."

"Never count on anything turnin' up but your toes."

"Poverty an' gratitude never go hand in hand."

"One reason why you can't allus git a business man interested in reform, is that th' better people are, th' less they spend."

When Kin got ready to satirize the ponderous, often ambiguous and pretentious economic forecasts by the Federal Government, he appropriately chose Tell Binkley as his spokesman.

THE ICE-CREAM CONE vs. THE LEGITIMATE CHANNELS OF TRADE

EX-CASHIER TELL BINKLEY

Owing to the tendency of the times it is peculiarly difficult to foresee with any degree of accuracy what may happen in 1909. The year will undoubtedly contain the usual twelve months and will comprise the latter part of the 133d and the beginning of the 134th year of American Independence and New Year's Day will be the 2,417,579th day since the beginning of the Julian Period.

While it is generally conceded that the business stagnation which is general the country over as I write has been brought about by the President's crusade against dishonesty in high places, I have at hand many expressions to the contrary by a multitude of distinguished thinkers, and men well up in the councils of the nation. It is the opinion of some that the gulf stream is changing its course; that the ice-cream cone is taking millions out of the legitimate channels of trade; that the moral wave is causing many more thousands to be taken from the tills of the rumshops, and conveying them into the hands of poverty stricken mothers and children, who in turn place them with the nickel theater; that the abolition of the saloon in many localities has only caused many men to tighten up that paid their bills when flushed with wine. In these calculations the argument is also made that the growing disposition to own an automobile after making only one payment is in no small degree causing much uneasiness in business circles. Our panic has been a deplorable thing and to my own knowledge no less than eighteen hundred people were caught that had just made their first payment on a rug or piano. What will become of them unless confidence is restored is only to be conjectured.

In the face of all the complications of the present time I do not deem it advisable to offer any prognostications bearing either on earthly or astronomical affairs.

Uncle Niles Turner

Uncle Niles Turner is Bloom Center's eldest senior citizen. He's just a trifle over 103. He accounts for his age by saying that he has always smoked, and chewed tobacco, and stayed away from lawyers. On the other hand, he says that if he had abstained from tobacco he would be at least 150. Uncle Niles delights to while away the evening of his life telling the most outrageous and preposterous Indian stories, and scaring little children. He's just a hearty, nostalgic, crusty old-timer with a remarkable memory and little or no regard for the truth.

Kin Hubbard was keenly aware of a great gap in understanding between the younger and the older generations in the country. When he wanted to comment satirically on this matter, no one could be a better spokesman for him, at least on one side of the question, than his old-timer, Uncle Niles Turner.

T'DAY'S GIRL

UNCLE NILES TURNER

When th' average mother gits t' reviewin' th' past she can't help comparin' th' pleasures an' opportunities o' t'day with th' slow goin' commonplace diversions o' her uneventful girlhood. So she sets on th' verandy in th' evenin' an' smiles an' quietly congratulates her daughter as th' tender striplin' hops int' a mouse colored six-cylinder juggernaut an' spins away in a cloud o' cigarette smoke with some irresponsible pompadoured caterpillar. "Let th' poor child enjoy herself while she kin fer she'll be married soon enough." That's th' modern mother's instinct croppin' out, but it haint th' motherly instinct o' th' ole Plymouth Rock hen that never loses sight o' her chicks till they are feathered out an' on a payin' basis.

TH' MODERN GIRL WOULD STEP ON A CAMEL IF ONE WUZ WAITIN'.

Our girls are growin' up too fast. We no longer see th' meekness that used t' lurk under th' long lashes o' Miss Sixteen. . . . We miss th' ole indescribable somethin' about th' girl in her teens that used t' make us stutter an' tremble in her presence. We wonder if she's gittin' all th' home trainin' that's comin' t' her. . . . What is your daughter readin'? "Vanity Fair" er "Deserted on Her Weddin' Morn." Is she singin' "Sweet Genevieve" er "Mingle Your Eyebrows With Mine"? Does she leave anythin' fer th' imagination when she dresses up? . . . . Is ther a photo o' a youth leanin' agin th' talcum can on her dresser? If ther is, study th' necktie an' hair cut carefully before it's too late. . . .

And what about th' huggin an' th' pettin' that t'day's girl is faced with? Huggin' an' pettin' used t' take place, in a modest way, in th' dimly-lighted parlor or on th' vine-hidden porch swing. But nowadays in any social assemblage, some mush heads jist can't keep from clawin' every woman they meet. They paw every bare back an' every bare arm they see. Our women's an' girl's backs an' arms are gittin' as slick an' as hard as a bannister. An' th' worst of it is, our women and girls don't seem t' resist rubbin' an' pattin'. I've seen 'em back up to it! I guess they're afraid t' shrink fer fear o' bein' called cattish an' cold; or maybe they jist regard open fondlin' as one of th' liberal movements of th' day. But marriage is goin' t' be an awful comedown fer th' girl that's been squeezed an' petted all th' time. After th' honeymoon fades away, her husband'll begin t' cool down, and examine her mind. An' he'll expect t' find some intellectual qualities t' tide him over an occasional long, draggy evenin' at home. An' what if ther hain't none? . . .

But after all's said ther's much t' admire in t'day's girl, her pluck, her effort t' be selfsustainin', an' her aversion t' dishwater an' cannin' t'maters. She hustles out an' goes t' work even tho' economic conditions don't demand it. I love t' see her after th' business worries o' th' day start fer home with her nose in th' air. I like her assurance, th' way she hops a car, or steps in an' auto. She'd step on a camel, too, if one wuz waitin'. She don't seem t' care how high she steps. . . .

Father is th' one t' talk t' daughter. Let him fergit his own diversions an' interests fer a spell each day an' try an' locate his daughter, th' little girl who used t' set on his knee an' ask t' see his watch, or his gold teeth, an' tell her somethin' o' th' snares an' pitfalls o' life, tell her that self-respect an' a clear conscience amount t' more'n all th' fur coats an' metal helmets in th' world piled t'gether, an' that ther's many a heavy heart beats behind a gin buck.

Miss Mame Moon

Mame Moon is muddling along in her middle forties, or thereabouts. She is square-jawed, muscular, and massive— truly a Clydesdale woman. Mame is owner and proprietor of the local Star Livery Stable as well as the O.K. Used Car Lot. She is also a powerful speaker and a fearless champion of universal women's rights.

When Kin Hubbard wanted to make comments on the subject of "emancipated women," he frequently called on Miss Mame Moon to speak for him. And often he placed Mame in a public speaking situation. In this instance, Mame addresses the local all-women Shakespeare Club.

LEAP YEAR

MISS MAME MOON

"This is leap year an' I reckon a girl kin propose t' a young man with impunity. Ther's allus been leap years, but I doubt if any o' us ever knowed a case where any girl ever actually took advantage o' th' privelege an' asked any feller point blank t' marry her. Ther's allus been a lot o' hintin' an' beatin' around th' bush an' hypnotizin' an' vampin', but I don't believe any girl ever blurted out a straight proposal. But now that we've been emancipated, I look fer a lot o' radical changes. Women an' girls are makin' big money an' votin' an' smokin' an' joinin' organizations like th' men an' have as much t' lose by gittin' married as th' men. I don't see why a girl that owns her own home an' makes big wages an' has money in th' bank shouldn' cast about fer a man o' her likin'. Th' marriage business has allus been too one-sided. A feller 'll start out an' trifle away th' time of a half dozen girls before he finds one that suits him. Sometimes he'll take up a girl's time fer years an' suddenly leave her on th' market all shop worn an' faded an' turn t' some other girl an' marry her in a week. A man never despairs an' gits desperate an' marries any ole girl, but many a girl has done that very thing. Why? Because she wuzn' priveledged t' pick out a man an' propose t' him before her chances went glimmerin'. Now that all things are equal I look for a different order o' things. After a girl gits well located in life an' has bright prospects an' feels a loneliness comin' over her she should git out an' select a husband. Women have been hangin' back an' standin' around waitin' like a lot o' produce in a market stall waitin' fer customers. They've allus had t' take what come along. Maybe they'd draw a husband with money an' maybe they wouldn', maybe they'd draw a good poor husband or a rich brute, maybe they'd draw some feller jest gittin' on his feet, or some feller that wuz flourishin'. But in nearly ever' case ther's been somethin' missin' that wuz essential t' real drawn out bliss. But t'day, with all her liberty, her opportunities an' resources, ther'll be blamed little sympathy fer th' girl that marries a lemon. T'day's girl, with her independence an' ever' avenue open t' her, kin at last marry any kind of a feller she likes. Let her go leisurely about it, let her select a man jest like a man picks out a automobile. Let her snoop around among th' various brands o' men an' choose th' one she thinks she kin afford."

Kin Hubbard saw advertising in magazines become big business and was dismayed by how some magazine publishers changed the essential quality of their magazines by crowding out or changing the aims of literary and informational materials in order to accommodate a greater number of unseemly types of advertisements. In this instance, Miss Mame Moon seemed to be just the right character to express resoundingly what Kin wanted to say on the subject.

WOMEN'S LEGS AN' ADVERTISIN'

MISS MAME MOON

Th' present day exploitation o' women's legs fer ever' conceivable sort o' advertisin' shows th' trend o' th' American mind. Seventy-seven out o' eighty-one advertisements in a current magazine were illustrated by women's legs in some shape or other, crossed, or kickin' up, or in repose. No magazine story is complete without a flapper curled up on a davenport showin' a pair o' legs. No Sunday newspaper is complete without a page full o' Miammy Beach, or Atlantic City legs. It's amazin' how darin' women become jest th' minute they hit a bathin' resort. I hain't heard o' one endurin' romance that begun below th' thighs. . . . One could think that men would git tired o' lookin' at legs, unless a pair o' shapely ones come along, which is hardly likely, but they rubber as bad as they ever did. But what I started in t' remonstrate agin is th' shameless way our legs are bein' used t' advertise citrus farms in the Rio Grande valley, vacations in Honolulu, hog cholera cures, auto bodies, humidors, roup remedies, tuna fishing, fertilizers, glaciers, tooth brushes, roach paste, Airedale pups an' trips t' th' Holy Land. Even a skid chain ad is not complete without showin' a pair o' our legs stickin' out o' an auto wreck. Miss Tawney Apple wuz offered $10 t' put on a bathin' suit an' pose fer an old home week ad. A photergraph o' th' way women an' girls sit around t'day with ther legs crossed smokin' cigarettes would have been barred from th' mails a few years ago. Man used t' look forward t' th' March winds, an' policemen used t' club 'em off o' prominent windswept corners, but things have changed. I guess exposed legs an' knees belong t' th' times th' same as wife tradin', gin, big alimony, Seminole pajamas, an' th' corn borer.

Mame Moon also once said:

Women never git th' benefit o' th' doubt. If they don't look good they might as well be bad.

And there was an interesting news item in the Sliphorn *about Mame:*

Miss Mame Moon who wuz jugged Monday fer blockin' the sidewalk in front o' th' pust-office, has been invited t' address th' Ladies Ballet Society o' Rochedale, if she gits arrested agin.

Mrs. Tilford Moots

Mrs. Tilford Moots is fifty, all right, but looks considerably older. She is a frail, weary farm wife. Tilford Moots's wife does the household chores, raises the kids, cooks, sews, helps with the ploughing, seeding, and haying. But that's not all. She also markets most of the fruits and vegetables she raises. What's left she cooks up and transforms into countless tidy rows of canned vegetables, jellies, jams, and pickles. Occasionally Mrs. Moots flees the farm for a hasty Grange supper or a brief winter's meeting with the Art Embroidery Club of Bloom Center.

Mr. and Mrs. Tilford Moots went to Niagara Falls for their honeymoon. That was it. Mrs. Moots has a little money saved that she wears in a chamois-skin purse around her neck, just in case.

Kin Hubbard probably never used the phrase "abused women," but he knew much about the meaning of the term. In many of the sayings and in a number of Short Furrows he designates the housewife on a farm as the most abused woman of his time. Ironically, but fittingly and effectively, he lets Mrs. Tilford Moots and her neighbor, Mrs. Jake Bentley, tell their own stories about what a woman's life might be like on a farm.

MRS. TILFORD MOOTS' REMINISCENCES

Ther's been an awful change in house cleanin' since I wuz first married. T'day you jest run over th' furniture with a oiled rag, shake a few rugs, an' run th' vaccum back o' th' Victroly, an' the job's done. I wish I had a nickel fer ever' time I carried a stove out t' th' barn. I had a beautiful back when I wuz first married, but it begun t' sag with my first house cleanin'. I heerd somethin' crack th' first time I tried t' lift th' bureau an' kick th' carpet out from under it, an' my back got round from then on. I used t' shove th' furniture from one room t' another at house cleanin' time. Then I'd pull th' carpet tacks an' take up th' carpet an' hang it out t' beat. Then I'd take th' straw off th' floor an' burn it.

Then I'd shovel th' dirt out. Then I'd scrub th' floor with soft soap. Th' funny thing about it all is that when I look back I can't see my husband anywhere. I don't remember o' him ever bein' around even when I carried th' stove out t' th' barn. I cleaned all th' rooms th' same way. When I'd carry th' stoves out t' th' barn I'd grease 'em t' keep 'em from rustin'. In th' fall I'd polish 'em, an' carry 'em back. I recall how I flushed with pride when my husband would look at 'em admirin'ly an' say, "Hello, you've bought some new stoves." Tackin' down carpets wuz a terrible job. What movin' bureaus an' carrin' stoves didn' to t' my form th' carpet stretcher did. Th' most villainous implement ever introduced int' th' home wuz th' carpet stretcher. I'd rather whitewash a dozen ceilin's than touch one. You couldn't have purty knees an' put down a carpet. It took all th' sponginess out o' mine. It wuz a pleasure t' wash lace curtains an' hook 'em on th' stretchin' frames an' I never tired o' it, an it wuz a little pleasant diversion t' walk down t' th' livery stable an' git th' bed ticks filled with straw an' carry 'em home. You'd allus meet somebuddy you knew t' talk to. But puttin' down a carpet flattened your knees an' threw ever' line in your body out o' gear. Ever bed slat in th' house used t' be scrubbed separately an' stood in th' sun t' dry. I have allus loved t' paint th' barn, but I never felt safe standin' on a rockin' chair an' hangin' a picture. My husband must surely have been around when I use t' move th' organ, but t' save my life I can't remember it. Th' organ wuz as heavy as a safe an' had no casters, an ther wuz jest a certain way it would go thro' th' hall door. Then I allus repapered th' wood box twice a year, an' cleaned th' cistern. Believe me, when I got thro' scrubbin' an' rubbin' an climbin' an' crawlin' an' tuggin' an' whitewashin' an' stretchin' an' tackin' our home smelled like a clean towel. I recall so vividly how proud I used t' feel when my husband would turn up as if by magic, an' say, "Emmy, you're a great little girl. Here's some change; buy yourself a new calico dress. I want you t' look like other women."

And here Kin Hubbard has Mrs. Jake Bentley not so much remin- isce as talk straight out about a woman on the farm.

WOMAN ON TH' FARM

MRS. JAKE BENTLEY

I don't think woman wuz ever cut out fer farm work, an' I think th' headstones in Tharps Run cemetery 'll bear me out. She hain't muscled fer it, an her instincts are finer than a male's, an' not adopted t' hog raisin', grubbin' an' manure spreadin'. Splittin' wood an' plowin' throw a woman's contour out o' drawin'. Mebbe foolin' with chickens, an' even a little moderate churnin', are harmless diversions that may not enhance feminine beauty, or stimulate woman's intellectual qualities, but they do no particular harm. On th' modern, well equipped farm, drudgery has been practically eliminated, an' ther remains little t' do that kin be said t' retard th' intellectual advancement, or warp th' frame o' th' farmer's wife, 'cept th' plowin'. I kin recall when a farmer picked out a wife jest like he picked out a work horse. He'd walk 'round her two or three times an' size her up. Mebbe he'd pinch her arms, or look at her teeth, or trot her back an' forth a few times, an' then listen t' her breathin'. He wuz lookin' fer a partner that could grub some new land, or ditch a meadow, or slop hogs. Pickin' out a wife fer farm work wuz a purely business proposition. Th' ole time farmer wanted a good, sound draft wife, one that wuz gentle an' ploddin' an' wouldn' scare—a woman any farmer could drive. Lon Moon's father wore out four wives before he got his farm in good shape. His fifth wife got scared an' ran off th' day he started t' grub a wild plum thicket. He wrote t' her an' promised t' put a pump in th' kitchen if she'd return, but his letter came back unopened.

Hon. Ex-Editor Cale Fluhart

Editor Cale Fluhart is a hale 85. He's the vigorous, inquisitive, blustery, and censorious editor and publisher of the *Bloom Center Weekly Sliphorn.* Folks in Bloom Center mostly regard the *Sliphorn* as a lively, gossipy newspaper such as any well-ordered country town needs. Cale boasts that the *Sliphorn* is a newspaper with a conscience! And Cale is known throughout Brown County for his wise yet fiery editorials. In his paper Cale keeps the citizens of Bloom Center well informed about town affairs, and he pumps hard for the things he personally thinks will improve the town and county. There's much ado in the *Sliphorn* about state and national politics, too, especially on election years. However, although Cale is known to be an incorrigible Democrat, he hedges a little about the political allegiance of the *Sliphorn,* so's to hold a decent number of Republican subscribers.

Cale is deservedly proud of his newspaper. But every so often he runs a contest for his subscribers to find out what they like best about the *Sliphorn.* Or maybe the contest is to find out if anyone is even reading his paper. Readers that enter his contests usually respond in an interesting variety of ways. For instance:

I like the *Weekly Sliphorn* because:

"It has a whole week to sort out what's fit to print."—Turpin Pusey

"It has never hesitated to be on the popular side of a question, regardless of its own opinion."—Clem Harner

"I like the *Sliphorn's* way of sayin' nothin', yet writin' at length."—Artie Small

"I like the *Weekly Sliphorn* best of all because it fits the pantry shelf."—Angie Moots

To make the *Sliphorn* lively and informative enough to grab and hold the interest of all its readers, Cale each week prints a lot that's just for and about local people. Fawn Lippincut, as we know, writes a number of feature columns. And of course activities of all civic and social organizations are reported. But apparently the stuff in the *Sliphorn* that most tantalizingly appeals to many readers is found in the many columns of "personals" that Cale dutifully publishes each week.

Miss Zazette Pash was married at noon yesterday to Lester White. She wore a gown of pearl tulle with beads of perspiration to match.

It's been just a year ago today since Mrs. Windsor Kale went to the altar supported by her father and he's still supporting her.

Doc Mopps and the boys are back from a hunting trip in Arkansas. They killed six quarts.

Tiry Buff is takin' his wife's vacation.

Poor ole Turpin Pusey hez hed a pick o' trouble. His wife wuz struck by lightnin' while she wuz plowin', three sons takin' th' gold cure, an' a dorter thet recites.

Pinky Kerr says thet th' difference between a trained seal an' a regular actor is thet yer hev t' feed th' seal.

Mrs. Ike Lark forgot and left her grandpa on the porch overnight.

Mrs. Lafe Bud attended court all Wednesday morning. As she left, she was heard to remark: "The feller that shoots his wife, and then kills himself, must feel cheap when his wife recovers!"

Ike Moon will be operated on tomorrow. He will leave a wife and three children.

If you read the *Sliphorn* you just know that Cale Fluhart believes an editor should partake fully in the life of the community he serves. And Cale does. He's a member of every legitimate and respectable organization in town, and some borderline outfits, and he's available without any urging to speak on a wide range of social, intellectual, or political subjects.

Many years have passed since Ex-Editor Cale Fluhart came to Brown County and established the *Bloom Center Weekly Sliphorn*. He now makes a big noise around town, and so is content. He says, "A feller that's prominent in a small town ought to stay there."

Kin Hubbard was a persistent, serious student of politics and like his father before him, an ardent life-long Democrat. In 1928, the Democratic party nominated Al Smith, a Catholic and four-time Governor of New York State, as their candidate for President. Al Smith lost the election to Calvin Coolidge. In 1929 Kin felt compelled to review some of the recent actions of the Democratic party and comment on the current general state of politics in the country. For this frank, outspoken essay on politics he appropriately gave the by-line to Ex-Editor Cale Fluhart, already known to readers as being very concerned and articulate about such matters. In some ways it does seem that when Kin created Editor Cale Fluhart he had in mind his father, Thomas Hubbard, Editor of the Bellefontaine (Ohio) Examiner.

THE PARTY OF JEFFERSON
HON. EX-EDITOR CALE FLUHART

While the Democratic party holds out the only hope o' return o' the fundamental principles on which this country wuz built, an' as a result o' which it has flourished, the fact remains that it has got to change its style of pitchin' if it ever expects to git anywhere. The result o' the last presidential election shows that the country is in no mood to be reformed. The party made a mistake in foolin' with the Eighteenth Amendment. Now that ever'buddy makes his own gin an' beer, ther's no longer any interest in the wet an' dry issue. Nothin' kin be gathered from the late tremendous hail o' ballots to show that the country is in the least way concerned about graft an' crookedness. That issue is as dead as the tariff. What did the Democratic party ever git out o' stickin' up fer the rights o' the workin' man 'cept to git ever' employer in the country arrayed against it? The workin' man either fergits to vote, or votes fer protection against "the pauper labor o' Europe." Some o' the wise heads an' long whiskers o' the Democratic party thought all the women would vote fer Smith 'cause they wuz tired washin' beer bottles, but what did we find? The women who wuzn' fer Smith on account o' his religion wuz again' him because his wife had raised a large family an' is still comely. Our party made a play fer the man in the street, an' it might jest as well have tried to appeal to the bottle capper manufacturers. Honesty in public office wuz another cry our party put up only to learn that nobuddy is interested in honesty in office. Another thing that defeated us wuz this—the election caught the country jest at a time when most voters wuz payin' on ther cars, an' wuz afraid to make a change. If Al Smith had come out an' promised not to change anything but a few pustmasters ther'd be a different tale to tell. Al Smith is lively an' snappy, an' the wonderful nation-wide confidence in Coolidge shows that the country likes a quiet, obscure president. All it wants is a new newspaper picture of its president ever' day or two jest to show that the gover'ment at Washin'ton still lives. The Democratic party don't do enough winkin'. It's too serious fer this frivolous age. But the most glarin' mistake our party made wuz takin' up with the farmer after its experience with the labor vote. A farmer is a Republican fer the same reason he's a farmer, an' not even a famine can change him. I hope the party'll have sense enough never again to take up the troubles of any class. It's a well-known fact that downtrodden people are famous fer bein' ungrateful. The Democratic party is still alive an' powerful. All it lacks is cunnin', an' about three or four hundred good newspapers an' magazines instead o' two or three.

Throughout his work Kin Hubbard used Editor Cale Fluhart and the Bloom Center Weekly Sliphorn *in many interesting ways. Here, in what purports to be an editorial by Cale Fluhart, Kin gets to comment on something that was a frequent target for his satire.*

Editorial

INTELLECTUAL VANITY

CALE FLUHART

A little dash o' vanity is jest as essential t' a well ordered individual as a good firm spine or a light runnin' liver. Th' proper amount o' vanity makes us perk up an' desire t' excel rather than bein' called jest a good hard workin' feller. It inspires us t' hold ourselves t' a strict accountability. Without a certain amount o' vanity we'd neglect t' git our necks shaved. We'd begin t' sag early in life an' take t' th' alleys rather than hunt up a clean collar. We'd soon fall a prey t' th' allurments o' th' livery barn an' shun th' cleaner walks o' life. But th' egotist—th' intellectually vain, th' stuck up, th' upstart! Of all th' varied abominations that infest th' terrestrial globe ther is nothin' t' compare with him. Self-centered, self-satisfied, pompous, overbearin', marvelous, unparalleled—he finally becomes too great t' bathe, when he is scented an' avoided.— From *Th' Bloom Center Weekly Slip Horn.*

Constable Newt Plum

Newt Plum is a bulky 50, or so. He is *the* honest, conscientious, and amiable officer of the law in Bloom Center. Newt's a little slow in thought and action; nevertheless, he's an inspiring sample of what a good, calculating, upright gentleman of steady habits, a strong right arm, and a disposition "to do" can accomplish in a small community like Bloom Center that offers all too few advantages.

After some disappointing experiences in higher education when he was young, Newt headed out West where he worked for a while at odd jobs. He finally drifted into Brown County, and being a fellow who could drink or leave it alone, he soon got into politics. Luckily, hitting an off year, he was nominated and elected constable, a position he has held for over 30 years. Constable Plum has been unfailingly devoted to the duties of his office. He has gamely tried to keep peace and order in the streets and homes of Bloom Center. He runs a clean and orderly log jail. And when Constable Plum gives orders down at the jail, or argues fine points of the law, the thunder of his voice easily carries throughout the town—sometimes into the surrounding countryside. Newt thinks his prime responsibility is to keep Bloom Center and all of Brown County fully informed about whatever is the current state of crime in town or county. And so it follows that Newt, by voice or in print, is constantly informing and warning the whole community about the horrifying rise in the rate of crime. As Newt cries out for help in his valiant fight for law and order, he frequently has to complain about the aggravating apathy of a public that shirks any responsibility for helping in the betterment of local, state, or national affairs.

Constable Newt Plum frequently became Kin Hubbard's spokesman during the 1920s when Kin chose to comment on the rising rate of crime, or about law and justice.

THE PUBLIC'S ATTITUDE TOWARD PROHIBITION

AN ADDRESS BY CONSTABLE NEWT PLUM

"If a bank is robbed by outside parties th' public gasps, it's aroused. Citizens turn out an' help hunt th' bandit. . . . We'll git forty different discriptions o' th' bandit by folks that seen him, an' th' whole state 'll git excited an' indignant. But if I find a fifty-gallon still a low mumble goes up an' I can't git a word out o' nobuddy. I can't even borrow a team t' haul it t' jail. . . .

"Ever' time I nab a rum runner en route I know perfectly well that I'm goin' t' spoil a convention, or throw a cold blanket o'er some house party.

"I know of a weddin' in this town that wuz called off 'cause I stopped a car an' confiscated an extry tire filled with white mule.

"I seized a big parlor lamp full o' white mule in a prominent home here that wuz so powerful one could etch his name on a knife blade with it. I saved th' family's life, but it's done ever'thing t' defeat me at th' polls.

"A dry enforcement officer kin never expect t' git any higher. . . .

"If a bootlegger sold t' bums an' people o' no standin' we'd have th' jail full o' them in a week. . . .

"Some fellers are great sticklers fer law enforcement till I arrest ther wives.

"It gives a town a bad name t' stop ever' car that goes thro' it, so I only aim t' stop half th' cars, thereby confiscatin' only fifty per cent o' all th' liquor that passes thro'.

"Jesse James' neighbors, good God-fearin' farmers an' ranchmen, used t' protect him, an' it's th' same with our bootleggers.

"Th' last bootlegger I got after I run fourteen miles in th' wrong direction, due t' faulty information."

When Kin was ready to expose to ridicule some of the many theories about what might be causing all the crime across the country in the 1920s, Constable Plum again admirably served him in a simple forthright manner.

CRIMINALS AN' HOME TRAININ'

CONSTABLE PLUM

I want t' bitterly ridicule th' conclusion recently arrived at by th' International Conference of Police Chiefs that lack o' home trainin' is responsible fer our criminals. In so fer as regards that's concerned, ther hain't nothin' into it. . . . Th' worse defaulters an' sharpers an' sneaks I've ever knowed had good folks. Some o' them wuz educated fer th' ministry, an' all o' them had been home trained right down t' th' minute. . . . Al Timmons's big auto wuz stolen by his own brother who'd never been away from home but once in his life. . . . O' course it's fine fer folks t' set a good example fer ther children an' urge 'em t' be honest so that when they git put in jail they feel like they'd done ther best t' train 'em. Pearl Slocum, that wuz electrocuted in th' east a few days ago fer murderin' an aged couple fer seventy cents, wore spectacles when he wuz a little boy an' recited in public. He had a goat an' a velocipede an' wuz a well trained normal boy an' didn' leave home t' go t' work till he wuz thirty-two. . . . Fer ever' brutal, clumsy crime committed by some dull ignorant feller of obscure origin, ther's ten well planned atrocious crimes committed by smart, educated an' responsible fiends with A-1 early trainin'. Jest recount th' crimes o' th' last few months that wuz committed by well connected, well raised an' even well-t'-do criminals. So well connected an' well-t'-do, in fact, that most of 'em are goin' free as fast as they're tried. Ther's some purty good an' substantial people in this country that didn' even have homes, t' say nothin' o' home trainin'. Also there's a lot o' well bred crooks that are gittin' by on account o' their splendid early environment. Let our police chiefs give more time t' roundin' up criminals an' not worry about how they originate.

Squire Marsh Swallow

Squire Marsh Swallow is pushing 80.
Alert, sharp, crotchety, for a long time
Judge Swallow has been known as the
most fearsome and fearless figure in the
local courthouse. After many years as a
struggling, impoverished small-town
attorney, Marsh Swallow acquired a local
reputation as a clever and tenacious trial
lawyer who rarely lost a criminal case.
When he finally ran for judge, he won by
a landslide. As a trial judge, Squire
Marsh Swallow handles criminal cases

with admirable dispatch, notably gives concise and curt instructions to
the jury and savage sentences to hardened criminals. Always
extremely impatient, the Judge becomes particularly disgruntled and
short-tempered when he sits in judgment on silly family altercations
or a long parade of trumped-up and unnecessary divorce cases.

TH' LICKLIDER DIVORCE CASE

SQUIRE MARSH SWALLOW

"Both o' you go on back home an' curb your tempers, an' you wash
th' paint off o' your mug. After a woman snares a husband ther's no
longer any excuse fer her daubin' her face up like a Cherokee Injun,"
roared 'Squire Marsh Swallow, this mornin', after listenin' t' Sue Licklider tell her side o' th' story in th' Licklider divorce case. Later 'Squire
Swallow said, "Th' outside world is gittin' t' believe my court is a
clearin' house fer lopsided marriages. I've split up quite a few couples
in th' last month, but I'm goin' t' call a halt. Women are so used t' takin'
things home on approval, an makin' things over, an' exchangin' things,
an' takin' things back, that they use th' same system with husbands.
They jest reason that they kin take a man an' if they don't like him
they kin dump him. Sometimes they try t' make him over. Men don't
hanker fer divorces as much as women do. They hain't home much, an'
besides they kin git away with a double life better'n a woman. A
woman 'll see another man she likes better, jest as she sees another
hat she likes better, but she rarely tries t' own 'em both. Lots o' men
think that if they give ther wives plenty o' spendin' money they're doin'
ther bit, but women want love an' affection an' money too. Ugly tempers is what mostly splits couples up. I've had couples before me that

wuz so homely an' rich that jealousy or money matters would be th' last thing in th' world t' split 'em up, then I'd find out that it wuz her temper or his temper that wuz comin' between 'em. These tempers show up in th' mornin's. If such couples would jist keep away from one another till eight thirty, or nine o'clock, they could worry thro' th' rest o' th' day all O.K., but it's tryin' t' eat breakfast t'gether that destroys ther happiness. I've told this Licklider t' git his breakfast down town till he gits better acquainted with his wife. They wuz only married last Saturday after goin' t'gether three hours. Then ther's another trouble—gittin' married too soon. A girl 'll git married before she's even seen her husband with his hat off, an' a fool of a boy 'll hook up with a girl without knowin' whether she's got any ears, or over one eye. This Licklider feller already owes a dental bill o' $81 his wife contracted since last Saturday. Couples that jump int' marriage should remember that each must give up somethin'—he's got t' give up his wages an' eat what he kin git, an' she's got t' give up paintin' an' stay at home occasionally. I'm thro' monkeyin' with 'em."

HUSBAND KILLIN'

SQUIRE MARSH SWALLOW

"Here is th' case of a reputable husband an' citizen bein' shot down without warnin' in his own dinin' room 'cause he wanted a straight up egg. He had lived with this murderess fer a year an' a half, givin' her ample time t' figure out how he liked his eggs. Competent witnesses have told us here that his preference fer straight up eggs wuz common knowledge, that no resturint in town would think o' servin' him a flopped egg," declared 'Squire Marsh Swallow, t'day, in summin' up th' evidence in th' Irene Mopps murder case. This case has caused wide comment on account o' th' flimsy provocation fer such a murder. It shows how cheaply th' lives o' husbands is held by modern wives. A few years ago before women dropped housekeepin' an' got into war work an' politics an' other downtown sports a husband could keep orderin' eggs till he got what he wanted. Wives used t' wait fer explanations, an' often ther wuz reconciliations, an' never nothin' worse'n estrangements an' divorces. . . . Husband murderin' has become so common that nobuddy looks up any more when a newsboy hollers, "Prominent husband bites th' dust!" Lots o' fellers that has aimed t' marry are reconsiderin' it. . . . Women are moody, but we've allus been able t' see a skillet or tea cup comin' in time t' sidestep, but a pistol's different. Husbands like t' live. Life holds lots o' things fer husbands, unless they've been married eight or nine years. An' we don't believe any woman kin be happy fer any reasonable stretch o' time after killin' a man, 'specially a husband that wuz good t' her a month or two at least. . . . Fixin' an egg is such a simple thing, so much easier than gittin' a new tailored suit made an' wadin' through a long tedious murder trial surrounded by a lot o' curious morbid people. O' course there's a nice way an' a brutal way t' order an egg, but so many girls jump in an' marry fellers thinkin' they're goin' t' board that no matter how a husband orders an egg in his own home he's takin' long chances.

Rev. Wiley Tanger

Rev. Wiley Tanger is slowly drifting toward 80. He is a solemn, slow-moving, dedicated, and occasionally inspired fundamentalist preacher who faithfully serves several parishes in Bloom Center and elsewhere in Brown County.

Rev. Tanger's good works in town are many. But he especially keeps busy visiting and freely giving counsel in the homes of *all* the townspeople: the healthy and the sick, the rich and the poor, the saved and the forsaken. He often drops in just in time to be invited for supper. And from the pulpit and in the home, Rev. Tanger constantly warns parents about the pitfalls and tribulations ever present in the proper moral upbringing of children.

Because of his sterling reputation for eloquence, Rev. Tanger has been asked to deliver countless graduation addresses for grammar schools and high schools throughout Brown County. He refuses a fee for such labors but sometimes will accept a modest "in kind" payment. One year, for his graduation address at Jerusalem High School, it is said that Rev. Tanger received three bushels of freshly-dug turnips, thirty-nine jars of elderberry jelly, one rhubarb pie (which he returned), and a hogshead of cider marked "for medicinal purposes only."

A life-long resident, and a constant mover for good in Bloom Center, Rev. Wiley Tanger perhaps understands the heart and soul of his home town better than any man alive.

Rev. Wiley Tanger has a modest share of idiosyncracies, which keep him keyed to the comic. But Kin Hubbard most often uses him as his spokesman for simple, essentially serious essays or for pieces that pleasantly, with gentle humor, summon up memories of a bygone day.

TH' LITTLE TOWN

REV. WILEY TANGER

Stew Nugent is at home t' put his feet under his mother's table. He has been t' th' city fer three years an' says that th' trouble with a little town is that ever'buddy knows ever'buddy else's business. That's th' reason Stew went away, an' it's one o' th' best things about a little town. You know who your next door neighbor is, an' you know who lives over th' hardware store. An' you know who's able t' own a tourin' car.

In a city where you don't need no other credentials but a good front it's different. Some folks flourish in a city that couldn't git trust fer a box o' corn flakes in ther home town. Some fellers apologize fer livin' in a little town. When you ask 'em where ther from they color up an' stammer an' say, "I—er—why—I—I'm from Rossville—that is my folks live ther. I've been livin' ther too, but I'm thinkin' o' goin' t' Chicago. There's no opportunities in a little town fer a young man." An' when you size him up you can't help picturin' what a flurry he'll cause in Chicago. O' course some folks that go t' th' city succeed, but they've got th' ole home metal in 'em.

In th' great city parks th' benches are filled with poor unfortunates from th' little towns who have tried an' failed. Pride alone keeps 'em from returnin' an' they become aimless wanderers an' are lost an' fergotten in th' mist o' time.

Some folks jist seem t' be cut out fer th' artificiality o' th' city, an' that's where they ought t' live. But if you want t' live an honest, quiet, peaceful life an' enjoy th' love an' confidence o' your friends an' neighbors, ther's no place like th' little town where one-half th' people knows how th' other half lives, where respectability is a real asset, where a K. of P. watch charm won't save you if you can't toe th' mark, an' where you're remembered long after th' hearse gits back t' th' livery stable.

TH' SLATY HOLLER COMMENCEMENT

Th' Slaty Holler school closed Wednesday fer th' plowin' season after a fruitful term. Th' graduation class consisted o' Evy May Bud, Artie Moots an' Clemmie Poole, an' what wuz lackin' in numbers wuz more'n made up in quality.

Rev. Wiley Tanger delivered th' baccalaureate address with much earnestness an' feelin'. He told th' graduates that what wuz commonly termed th' commencement wuz really th' biddin' good bye t' dear ole school days.

"You are settin' forth on th' sea o' life rich in knowledge an' penniless in experience. Th' rocks an' eddies are so arranged that only th' strongest hearts kin combat 'em. I want t' warn you agin th' thirst fer pleasure an' its decayin' effect on th' heart cells. Interest yourselves in politics till after th' primaries, even of you are workin'. In regard t' equal suffrage I will say that th' mother bird is safest in her nest an' that th' preservation o' our government depends on th' mother in th' home."

After takin' a couple o' flings at th' silhouette skirt an' th' mosquito bar stockin' . . . Rev. Tanger rested his case with th' follerin':

"Th' little bell in th' cupola has struck terror t' your hearts many times, but in after life, whether you have succeeded er failed, when its ole familiar tones are wafted back t' you at th' close o' life's fitful fever, you'll realize that th' fleetin' days o' school life formed th' happiest period o' your lives."

Prof. Alex Tansey, th' superintendent, in a few well chosen remarks impressed on th' graduates that life at its best in only a succession o' partin's, if not with friends er loved ones it's with money er somethin' else. . . .

"We Have Left th' Bay an' th' Ocean Lies Before Us" wuz th' subject o' Evy May Bud's essay. Her ears an' neck were spotless an' she looked ever' inch a sweet girl graduate. Her composition wuz a powerful one, an' you could almost hear th' waves as she described th' perils that awaited th' voyager after leavin' th' snug harbor o' th' school room.

Clemmie Poole's essay, "Th' Ethics o' Democracy," wuz heavy an' intellectual an' it wuz hard t' tell where he got it. He said th' French, er Rousseau, democracy antagonized th' puritan democracy an' Rooseveltian democracy, radically, systematically, vitally an' essentially, an' that obedience is axiomatic t' liberty. Even Professor Tansey admitted that what he said wuz jist like somethin' that seemed t' be th' better interpretation o' ethical democracy whether it wuz er not.

Artie Moots followed with an essay on "Th' Upkeep o' Popularity." He doubted th' value o' popularity as an asset. He said nobuddy could be popular without bein' imposed on, an' that ever' dollar gained thro' popularity cost eight dollars. He said popularity consisted chiefly in lettin' your friends use you, an' that an extremely popular person didn' enjoy enough privacy t' take a bath all over. . . .

Doctor Mopps, president o' th' school board, presented th' diplomas an' congratulated th' graduates on stickin' t' ther studies an' ther final triumph o'er three nickel the-aters. He said that education, however, wuz only a side line in th' struggle o' life—that hard work an' an agile liver were th' bulwarks agin which all later problems o' life are dashed t' pieces.

Doctor Mopps

Dr. Mopps is 89 going on 90 and, God willin', plans to zip to 100. He warns everyone in town not to use the phrase, "growing old." Dr. Mopps, genial, still alert and agile, has been fondly called "our family doctor" by generations of present-day and past families all over Brown County. He was born and raised in Chagrin Falls, Ohio, and was educated in the public schools of that fair and thriving hamlet. In the summers, during Doc's years of practical internship in medicine, he usually hung paper, or worked as a meat cutter in a hotel, or sold electric belts. Fresh from his medi-

cal apprenticeship to a distinguished surgeon of Cat Creek, Pennsylvania, Dr. Mopps came to Bloom Center in Brown County, where he put out his shingle to practice medicine, ran a livery stable on the side, and soon proved to be equally good at doctoring people, or horses, dogs, cats, hogs and cattle.

Right now, in the lingering autumn of his life, Dr. Mopps has slacked off considerably in his doctoring. But he tirelessly tends out on activities in the many social clubs to which he belongs, especially the Country Club. Furthermore, Dr. Mopps, always a popular public speaker and orator, is still in great demand for speeches and orations throughout Brown County.

Throughout his work Kin Hubbard often comes down hard on doctors and many aspects of the medical profession. Frequently Dr. Mopps's name or his actual presence enters the satire. In the public address by Dr. Mopps that follows, however, Kin Hubbard seems to be satirizing fatuous political oratory as much as he is Dr. Mopps and the medical profession.

TH' LIVER

DR. MOPPS

"Th' shameful treatment that is bein' accorded th' human liver in this day an' age is a reflection on our boasted civilization. We're rushin' ahead unitin' oceans, reducin' th' tariff, passin' currency bills an' checkin' hog cholera while th' great American liver struggles along doin' two livers' work without a friend in either branch o' Congress.

"Th' human liver (Swedish LEFVER) is a large light maroon colored digestive gland about the size of a catcher's glove that reposes in th' upper right hand corner o' th' abdominal cavity an', when conditions are as they should be, it weighs one-fortieth as much as th' body t' which it is attached. It is th' main gazabo o' th' human works but, notwithstandin' th' important role it plays in our pursuit o' life, liberty an' happiness, it is th' most abused, most misconstrued, most ignored, most imposed on, most neglected an' lied about organ of which th' medical fraternity has any knowledge.

"Next t' a yeller dog ther hain't nothin' that responds as readily t' kindness as th' human liver. Prunes, when properly stewed, are fine fer th' liver, but how many of us are darin' enough t' ask for them? We occasionally eat an apple jest t' please th' liver, but we rarely take th' liver int' our confidence when we attend a Jefferson Day banquet. We are not chummy enough with th' liver. How many of us have any knowledge of its plumbin'?

"A feller's disposition is regulated by his liver. Th' liver is th' switchboard o' his inclinations an' impulses. We often hear it said of a feller that he entered int' this er that with his whole heart. It wuz his whole liver. Most o' th' credit that goes t' th' heart rightfully belongs t' th' liver. . . .

"When th' human liver (Latin JECUR) is happly situated an th' lines leadin' therefrom are open t' traffic ther is nothin' that looks as bright an' beautiful as th' world."

Comments by Abe Martin

Mrs. Tilford Moots' niece wuz taken suddenly ill Monday an' died before Dr.
Mopps could git in from th' links.

> Nobuddy ever becomes so intelligent
> thet he can't be scared by a fake doctor.

Aunt Tabithy Plum says ther hain't
nothin' like goose grease and onions fer
babies. She ort t' know. She's buried
nine.

> Tilford Moots took his wife down t'
> Evansville Monday t' be operated on fer
> liveritis, an' t'day his niece got a letter
> sayin' thet th' operation wuz entirely
> successful an' thet th' body would be
> shipped home et once.

A New York doctor found a heart on th'
right side th' other day, which is some
luck fer a doctor.

A SHEAF OF SELECT
PIECES

*We have just seen a variety of Short Furrows that Kin Hubbard ac-
credited to Abe Martin's neighbors. Now we should look at several
special pieces or Short Furrows selected from the major divisions of
Kin's published materials. He wrote many pieces that stemmed from
his own early experiences or that described what small-town living
might be like in midwestern nineteenth-century America. Such works
might have appealed most to readers of Kin's age or older. On the other
hand, many of his finest comic pieces dealt with ideas or events that
presumably were of great current interest to most of his readers. Here
are a few selections from both categories.*

*In his later years Kin Hubbard vividly remembered the social at-
mosphere and some of the homely details of his early schooling in
Bellefontaine, Ohio. He set down his remembrances. The names he
used may be fictitious but the personalities, the schoolroom atmosphere, and the action described do seem authentic.*

OLE SCHOOLMATES

When I went t' school Albert Moore wuz th' best reader. He jist
seemed t' know ever'thing that McGuffey ever wrote an' he could quote
him by th' yard. He wuz th' leadin' man in all th' Friday afternoon
dialogues an' ever'buddy in town said, "That boy'll be a actor some
day." But he graduated an' caught th' first delivery wagon that come
along an' he's still one o' the' invaluable employees o' th' Star Laundry.

Mamie Turner wuz one o' 'em girls that allus walked home with th'
teacher an' combed her hair back till she looked like a chinaman an' her
forehead wuz full o' blue veins. She tattled ever'thing, too. . . .

Charley McCrea wuz a purty smart scholar an' made th' dandiest capital letters. Th' teacher allus got him t' write th' mottoes on th' blackboard, "Be Good an' You'll be Happy," an' "Dare t' do Right." He wuz jist cut out for a hut-tel clerk an' that's what he's loafin' at ever since he graduated. . . .

Gourdon Brown wuz th' smartest boy in school. He wuz a frail, little codger with a big square head an' younger than anybuddy in his class. His mother learned him at home but she cut his hair too high over th' ears. He wore spectacles an' a cape with a velvet collar an' jist seemed t' know ever'thing. . . . He'd cry if anybuddy else in th' class almost knew th' answer t' somethin'. He graduated an' fiddled around home a while an' disappeared. I seen him th' other day fer th' first time in thirty years. He's a big tall feller with sideburns an' had on a rubber collar an' a pair o' tan shoes dyed black fer November. He said he wuzn' doin' anything "these days." I wuz nearly crazy t' ask him what a archipelago wuz jist t' see if he'd remember.

A joyous event in Kin Hubbard's boyhood was the Logan County Fair, held each year in Bellefontaine, Ohio.

TH' OLE COUNTY FAIR

It seems like our blamed progressiveness is jist gradually takin' all th' flavor out o' th' ole time honored county fair. It wuz a great institution in th' days o' big pumpkins an' wholesome amusements. . . . Down in th' hollow, near th' main pump, Colonel Perry's Great Golden Museum and Educational Exposition had its tent. Th' Colonel wore a

AN AGRICULTURALIST AN' PRIZE HEIFER

wrong font plug hat an' long sidewhiskers an' his wife wore knee dresses, Roman sandals, an' took tickets an' lifted a cider barrel full o' water with her teeth an' did th' cookin'. In th' tent wuz a se-gar case full o' snakes an' a dried mermaid, an' Millie Irene, th' armless wonder, who wrote cards and crocheted lamp mats in colored yarn with her toes. She wrote a beautiful vertical foot an' ever' center table an' card receiver in th' county bore evidence o' her toe work.

I feel awful sorry fer th' feller that hain't got no ole delightful county fair days t' look back on.

Ever'buddy we used t' meet wuz savin' somethin' to' take t' th' fair. If it wuzn' a unusually big Shanghai rooster it wuz some crazy lookin' long necked gourd, an' if it wuzn' either o' 'em it wuz somethin' else crazy er unusual—maybe his wife, fer th' great annual agricultural exhibition used t' attract some awful odd lookin' folks. . . .

Kin Hubbard tapped his memory and imagination to record in vivid detail a slumberous midsummer's day during the third quarter of the nineteenth century.

DOG DAYS

When th' summer landscape takes on a scuffed an' faded appearance like a over exposed ten dollar suit we know we are face t' face with dog days, that midsummer season o' th' year when all livin' things jist sorter peter out an' languor rules supreme in shop an' mart an' field.

Th' brawny wage earner with muscles o' iron mopes about his work with a disposition t' do so much an' no more. Even folks with gilt edged livers succumb t' th' dull, warm monotony an' freely an' unreservedly express 'emselves as bein' utterly and unqualifiedly indifferent as t' whether school keeps er not. Even th' ideal wife sets th' succotash back t' simmer while she feels her way red an' faintin' t' th' verandy fer a little breathin' spell an' t' git a line on her neighbors.

In the dark cool parlor th' spider embroiders his filmy lace from th' crayon portrait o' grandma t' th' hangin' lamp with impunity. Th' upstairs smells like a lumber yard an' th' sewin machine is takin' a much needed rest. Th' birds have quit spoonin' an' ther fledglin's are scattered an' gone. Country butter is tinged with rag weed an' th' trousers o' your light suit are failin' fast, an' th' same ole hot, tortuous, dusty summer days come an' go with nothin' t' mar th' monotony but an occasional straw hat sale.

Dog days in a dressin' jacket town is th' nearest thing t' th' bottom o' a well when it comes t' peace an' quiet. Th' only things that enliven th' business section are a blue fly net an' a pile o' watermelons in front o' th' general store (th' season fer th' bright red cultivator with yeller runnin' gears havin' closed early in July). As th' sun rounds th' Baptist church steeple th' combination pustmaster an' storekeeper sprinkles th' melons an' fixes th' bell on th' screen door an' goes t' sleep near th' prunes. Across th' street under th' low boughs o' a wide spreadin' cottonwood tree in front o' th' Citizens' Bank th' oldest inhabitant curls up on a bench an' positively refuses t' be drawn out on th' Balkan war er th' currency question. At ten o'clock th' landlady o' th' Central House crosses th' road thro' th' dust in her bare feet carryin' a crock. At twelve th' dinner bells o' th' farms far across th' valley ring out an' th' livery stable keeper throws his terbacker out an' rinses his mouth at th' town pump an' goes home t' dinner. At three o'clock th' leadin' attorney emerges from his office over th' pool room with th' pockets o' his alpaca coat bulgin' with legal documents. Fillin' th' crown o' his hat with burdock leaves he ventures forth under th' wiltin' rays o' th' sun t' scare some farmer. As th' shades o' evenin' gather th' wheezy notes o' a clarinet come from th' open window o' th' bandroom an' die away in th' twilight. As th' constable sets his ladder agin' th' lamppost on th' public square, th' clatter o' hoofs is heard comin' o'er th' brow o' th' hill. Purty soon Steve an' Min in a side bar buggy pull up in front o' th' ice cream parlor, an' th' evenin's revelry begins. As they slowly wind their way home thro' th' quiet country lanes th' air is heavy with th' odor o' overripe alderberries an' dust. With one foot on th' dash board an' th' other danglin' carelessly on th' outside o' th' buggy, Steve throws th' lines around th' whip an' hugs Min passionately as she holds his hat an' implores him with all th' earnestness in her round husky makeup t' give up all notion o' th' Reg'lar Army an' stick on th' farm.

Abe Martin over the years had much to say about the striking changes in family life, leisure-time activities, and the social and economic status of individuals brought about by the enticing availability of the automobile for a multitude of Americans.

POOR AL MOON

My, how poor ole Al Moon fought fer a auto. He worked in th' same store from seven a.m. 'til six p.m. fer thirty years without even gittin' off fer a funeral er a ball game. He wuz what is generally known in th' business world as a invaluable employe. He made things hum at th' store, but he had t' smoke on th' porch at home. His wife wuz a thrifty little woman an' looked after th' Saturday disbursin' an' put ever'thing over actual operatin' expenses in a money doublin' scheme that wuz

headed by a feller that used to know her paw. Anybuddy could tell by th' way she pulled her hair back t' a knot that she wouldn' have nothin' t' do with an auto.

Al's salary wuz so triflin' that if he'd got it semi-annually in pig iron he could o' carried it all right. But his wife skimped till she bought 'em a home in th' kimona belt, an' he had to wear shirts that wuz only printed on one side an' socks with runnin' colors an' smoke a certain famous brand that come three in a pasteboard case.

He'd jist about lost all interest in life when he caught th' auto fever an' commenced t' send fer road maps an' circulars. One day he come home an' told his wife that he'd been workin' so long an' stickin' around home so much that his liver wuz off an' he had a warped view o' life, an' that he had decided t' git out an' see th' scenery while ther wuz yit time. His wife made him some burdock bitters n' put him t' bed. Th' next mornin' he told her that he didn't feel no better, an' that he intended t' mortgage th' home fer a six-passenger, fore door, forty horsepower Alice blue tourin' car with a five-inch stroke, four an' a half-inch long life motor, integrade clutch that run thro' oil, eliminated torsion bars an' distance rods, an' semi-elliptic forty-two inch front springs, an' that they could then wash up the mornin' dishes an' go ten miles a gallon with impunity.

After his wife recovered she told him he didn' have sense enough t' run a coffee urn er money enough t' afford a four-candle power porch light, an' she locked him in his room an' hid his stogies.

Poor ole Al. He never got out o' his room alive. He laid fer days with a high fever an' in his delirium he'd say, "Hey, there! Watch your horse an' never mind watchin' my auto." "How fer is Rensselaer?" "Ther goes a inner tube!" "Hop in Sam, an' I'll take you home," an' all sorts o' things. Jist before he died th' Johnsons that lived next door bought a fine big tourin' car an' when Al's wife found it out she rushed int' his room an' said, "Look up, Albert, it's Nettie, an' t'morrow we'll buy a machine." But she wuz too late.

As we journey thro' life let us live by th' way—even if we have t' mortgage th' ole home.

In the late 1920s many newspapers featured a long succession of front-page stories about lurid murder trials, replete with detailed accounts of senseless murders by fiendish methods and daily reports on the clever maneuvers of famous trial lawyers attempting to defend and free their criminal clients. On August 3, 1929, Kin Hubbard tried to clear the air of some unwholesomeness when he wrote his own account of a far-from-sensational criminal case conducted by a not-so-celebrated lawyer.

THE AMY PURVIANCE MURDER CASE

"Hain't you ever been kicked by a horse or fallen out of a haymow?" asked Pearl Curl, the celebrated criminal lawyer, of Mrs. Amy Purviance, in her cell at the County Jail.

"No, but my feet wuz froze onct when I wuz a girl, an' when I was little I drunk some lye, too," she replied.

Mrs. Purviance is charged with first-degree murder for killin' her husban' with a revolver, arsenic, an' a croquet mallet.

"Well," replied Attorney Curl, "We'll have to find a bump on you somewheres, or a streak of insanity, to save you from the noose. Have you any ancestors, an uncle, or gran'paw mebee, who wuz an inventor or writer, or an aunt or gran'maw who liked to hunt big game, or lived among the Indians? An' is ther any lien on the property you're turnin' over to me?"

"No, sir, the farm is as clear as a whistle, an' my ancestors wuz all normal I guess. Cept I have an uncle on mother's side who refused to sell his farm when he had a chance."

"Well, ther's two or three ways I think I kin save you from the noose, but you might have to stay almost a year in prison. The noose is the thing we want to look out fer, but a year's rest in prison never hurt nobuddy. What do you think o' emotional insanity? Or we might fix it up to have you out o' town when your husban' wuz killed."

"Yes, but I've confessed."

"Well, that won't hurt. We might show that he suicided if it wuzn' fer the d–d croquet mallet. You pulled a boner when you used that mallet. The mallet is goin' to make trouble. I like the emotional insanity plea the best, an' I think we'd better use it on account o' the mallet. Your husban' wuz all right wuzn' he—that is, he wuz a good husban' an' you had no provocation?"

"No, he wuz a good husban', only I got tired lookin' at him."

"I see. Did your mother ever drop you on a brick sidewalk when you wuz a baby? Suicide might make a good plea, but ther agin we run into the mallet. Did you have a mallet expectin' to use it, or was the mallet a second thought? O' course he could have swallowed arsenic an' he could have shot himself in the back. It's all nonsense to say a feller can't hold a revolver so's to hit himself any place he pleases. But he couldn't have killed himself with a croquet mallet. That would never occur to anybuddy no matter how tired o' life he wuz. What wuz the big idea in usin' the mallet? It might mean the noose for you. Have you ever been in trouble before?"

"I killed my paw, but it never got out."

"That's fine. Well, I'll go to work an' see if I can't work out somethin' along the line o' dementia Americana on account of the d–d croquet mallet. I'm goin' to make that mallet save you from the noose if I kin. I'll see you tomorrow, an don't talk."

Throughout his life Kin Hubbard maintained a strong belief in the validity of democratic governance, but sometimes he was strongly moved to express his frustration with the flawed way in which the democratic system sometimes works.

THE PEOPLE

We frequently hear references to "the people," what they're demandin', what they'll stand fer, an' what they won't. Who'er "the people," an' what are "the people"? The politician, or statesman, who assumes to know what "the people" want may know what he himself wants, or perhaps a few of his friends or neighbors want, but I don't think any livin' soul knows what "the people" want. The other day I heard a little pompous squirt say, "I'd like to know how long the people are goin' to stand fer it." I don't know whether he wuz talkin' about hijackin', or chuck-holes, or slim, straight legs, but whatever he referred to'll run its course jest the same as a "business man" Mayor, "Caroliny Moon," or the measles. Ther's times when a considerable number o' people'll become aroused an' club together an' hang some fiend to a telephone pole, or organize an' elect a reform mayor, but they soon split up an' git worked up over somethin' else. Ther hain't a minute o' the day that somebuddy hain't declarin' that "the people" want light beer an' wine, an' if it wuz put to a vote tomorrow ever' state in the Union would vote

THE PEOPLE IN ACTION

dry. Most o' "the people" have got their own stills an' beer-makin' apparatus, or prompt an' reliable bootleggers, an' anyhow few o' them would want to go back to anything as tame as beer or wine. Ever' so often a vast number o' people'll git aroused an' ther'll be a p'litical landslide. That's when we git our worst bunch o' office holders. "The people" are restless. They allus seem to want somethin', but they can't locate it. It's got so our statesmen don't know where they stand— idolized today an' afraid to come home from Washin'ton tomorrow. Stage favorites, social queens, new restaurants, reform administrations, an' blond trimmers, come an' have ther little whirl, an' are cast aside fer somethin' different. The public's jest like the ole-time kings we read about who laid around purple an' stupid from booze while anything that wuz likely to amuse 'em wuz rigged up an' trotted out. "The people" hain't only willin' to try anything once, but they're anxious. But ther's no limit to what "the people" 'll stand fer, an' theatrical producers, novelists, an' politicians found that out several years ago. The world must go on an' we must have changes, but ther's a whole lot o' fundamentals in this life "the people" ought to quit monkeyin' with, things they must git reconciled to an' make the best of. We mustn' git excited o'er what "the people" want, fer they don't know what they want. The thing to do is slip 'em what they ought to have, an' let 'em rave.

Over the years Kin Hubbard perforce had to listen to hundreds of speeches, including great quantities of pompous political and dedicatory oratory. As a satirist he knew just how to respond to his unhappy listening experiences.

THE PIONEER MOTHER

A monument to the pioneer mothers of America wuz unwrapped with fittin' ceremonies in the woods west o' the saw mill one day recently. Hon. Ex-Editur Cale Fluhart wuz the orator o' the occasion, an' among other things he said: "Our nation has been shamelessly remiss about doin' somethin' to perpetuate the memory o' the stalwart heroines who built up the great west. Too much has been written about Davy Crockett, Wild Bill, General Custer, Daniel Boone, an' other picturesque long-haired wing shots, an' scarcely anything about the brave, noble, dauntless wives, mothers, an' sweethearts who trudged across our continent in bunglesome, creakin' covered wagons drawn by bony, downcast oxen. There they sat, hemmed in by pots an' kettles an' bed clothes, an' mebbe a favorite bureau or cookstove, with ther eyes glued

A WELL EARNED MONUMENT

on the western horizon, while ther husbands stumbled along on foot an' prodded the slobberin' oxen. It is related o' the pioneer women that never once did they look back durin' the long, joltin', dusty, dangerous trip to the vast open spaces o' the west. The past, with all its joys an' comforts, its society, warm homes an' good eats, lay behind the brave, square-jawed women, fer they were ridin' toward a new day, they were follerin' the weary, bewhiskered, dusty, adventurous men they'd promised to love, honor an' obey. . . . Scarcely nothin' has been written about the tired, round-shouldered women, many of them mothers with five or six kids, who braved hardships durin' the winnin' o' the west. . . . They were dumped out on boundless prairies with nothin' to carry on with but an ax, a shovel, some pots an' kettles, an' a plow. They lived in sod houses. Often water wuz ten miles off. . . . Scarcely anything at all has been done by sculptors to play up the women who in the late '40s bade farewell to civilization, climbed on the front seat an' focused ther eyes on the settin' sun without even blinkin'. . . . Aside from a lot of gorgeous sunsets, what did our women ever git in return fer all they endured in the conquest o' the west?"

TH' OLE FAMILY CIRCLE

More'n once durin' our long hard blusterin' winter have I thought about th' old family circle we used t' see thro' th' windows as we trudged along th' street thro' th' snow in th' evenin'. Ther wuz mother an' th' girls an' father an' th' boys, all huddled around a big squatty lamp with a green shade in th' settin' room with real contentment written on ever' face. Mother knowed where her children wuz then, an' father wuz content with only one lodge. Ever'buddy knew what t' do with 'emselves in th' ole family circle days. Father had th' easiest chair on th' best side o' th' two leaf table an' read *Pilgrim's Progress*, er talked t' mother while she quilted er set th' buckwheat. Emmy made wax flowers er worked mottoes, while Alice got her algebra er sewed. Bob an' Henry played checkers on th' floor er poured over th' pages o' Daniel Boone er Robinson Crusoe. Ther wuz a big thick Bible on th' table, too, with th' pages cut. Ever'buddy wuz at home where they belonged.

Sunday wuz sparkin' day an' th' column stove in th' tidy little musty parlor wuz red hot from two in th' afternoon till ten in th' evenin', an' th' door leadin' in' th' settin' room wuz never closed, not because mother could not trust Emmy er Alice, but jist as a guarantee o' good faith. Bob an' Henry would shine ther boots an' git out new paper collars an' put oil o' bergamont on ther hair an' strike out, an' mother didn't worry no more'n if they'd jist gone down cellar after an apple.

These feverish days o' woman's clubs, cigarettes, cheap insurance lodges, the-ater goin', autos, an' suffragettes have destroyed th' ole family circle jist th' same as our civilization has destroyed th' Indians. It seems like ever'buddy from ten years up is lookin' fer a new sensation.

Call around t' most any modern home on th' coldest winter evenin' an' what do you find? Little Kenneth playin' with some blocks an' th' "maid" gossipin' o'er th' phone. Mother is addressin' a club, Violyette is blushin' at some musical show with a strugglin' clerk, Edythe is in a girls' seminary, Harold is in college preparin' himself fer some light employment, father has some important lodge work t' look after, an' nobuddy has seen Clarence fer two days.

Whether it's gentle spring, warm, lazy summer, golden autumn er cold bleak winter, th' modern family never gits t'gether any more unless ther's a funeral—an' even then ther's allus one missin'.

GOSSIP

MISS TAWNEY APPLE

We kin fortify ourselves agin a burglar er recover from a cheap plumber; we kin flee t' th' mountain an' avoid th' flood that sweeps th' lowlands er we kin muff a Wagner recital but there is positively no escape from a gossip.

"Ther goes Hattie Moon t' th' pustoffice agin jist as fast as her skirt'll let her. It's th' fifth time since ten o'clock. Is it any wonder decent people talk about her?" said Mrs. Tipton Bud t' Mrs. Tilford Moots this mornin'. Th' two women had stopped t' exchange reports on Art Simmons an' his new wife an' discuss th' possibility o' an early divorce.

Now th' truth is Hattie Moon is takin' stenography by mail with th' intention o' supportin' her widowed mother, but as she is purty an' stylish th' chances are she'll have t' git out o' town. Gittin' talked about is one o' th' penalties for bein' purty, while bein' above suspicion is about th' only compensation fer bein' homely.

Ever'buddy that hears a little dash o' gossip remounts it an' burnishes it up an' sends it on its way. If you try t' head it off you only stir it up. Nearly ever'buddy is more or less inclined t' gossip, but not allus maliciously. Folks gossip t' be interestin'. Th' fact that Ike Brown is a model husband an' pays his debts don't interest no one. Th' fact that his wife is a splendid good woman has no news value. But if you intimate that Ike Brown is on his last legs er that his wife has been visitin' her mother unusually long you have a crowd around you in a minute. Jist whisper t' some friend that a certain woman looks unhappy an' th' card clubs'll have her separated from her husband in a week.

An' gossippin' haint confined t' women an' little towns. Wherever ther's people ther's gossip. Clubs are clearin' houses fer gossip. Some clubs are organized fer historical research, some are organized t' better social conditions, some are organized t' combat certain evils, some are organized t' gamble fer stockin's an' pottery while others are organized fer purely social pleasure. Yet I doubt if anybuddy ever attended any kind o' a club meetin' without annexin' a little information o' a sensational nature.

Nobuddy's affairs ever demanded so much o' ther time that they couldn' give a little attention t' gossip. It's wonderful how much capacity some folks have—how easily they kin watch ever' detail o' their own business an' yours too.

A long nosed model housekeeper kin take her sewin' an' pull her rockin' chair up t' a side window an' see more thro' a pair o' ninety-eight-cent lace curtains than a Scotland Yard detective could find out in a year.

KIN HUBBARD,
ARTIST AS CARICATURIST

From Kin Hubbard's eight thousand or so drawings of Abe Martin and his neighbors, a thousand illustrations for the Short Furrows, and hundreds of dandy caricatures of state legislators and farm animals, everyone probably would like to choose his or her favorite compositions. With deep regret that such a delightful circumstance is not possible, and with great hope that each of you somehow will be pleased—and moved to laughter—the following choices are joyfully offered.

A SELECT FEW FROM THE GENERAL ASSEMBLY

ALEX TANSEY

THE YOUNG MISS FAWN LIPPINCUT

UNCLE ALEX NEWTON

BARTON CROSBY

TIPTON BUD

MRS. TIPTON BUD

LAFE BUD

MR. WES WHIPPLE

ABIGAIL AINSLEY

PINKY KERR

CONSTABLE NEWT PLUM

IKE LARK, BOOTLEGGER

CLEM HARNER

ELMER TITUS

MR. SCHUYLER WIGGINS

MISS GERM WILLIAMS

PROFESSOR ALEXANDER TANSEY

The End.

A SAMPLER ALMANACK

*A Miscellany of Selections
Gleaned from Various and
Sundry of the Twenty-Five
Annual Books of Kin Hubbard*

Abe Martin's Almanack

By Kin Hubbard

CONTAINING
TIMELY HINTS TO FARMERS AND YOUNG WOMEN
ACTUAL FACTS ABOUT THE MOON
ASTROLOGICAL LORE, TRUE EXPLANATION OF DREAMS
FAMOUS POLITICAL SPEECHES
RARE PHILOSOPHICAL MUSINGS AND MUCH
VALUABLE INFORMATION ALONG MANY LINES BY
SUCH NOTABLE MINDS AS
HON. EX-EDITOR CALE FLUHART
CONSTABLE NEWT PLUM AND HIS SON-IN-LAW,
PINKY KERR, TILFORD MOOTS
NILES TURNER, MISS FAWN LIPPINCUT
PROF. ALEX TANSEY AND DOCTOR MOPPS, ESQ.
TOGETHER WITH HUNDREDS OF
BRAND NEW EPIGRAMS
BY ABE MARTIN

With Illustrations by the Author

TO THOMAS EDWIN HUBBARD

Whose vocal gifts endear him to all our flat and who, wise beyond his one year, holds the chair of philosophy in the Abe Martin night school of tranquil thought.

KIN

Kin Hubbard! Why "Kin"? What does that "Kin" stand for? "Hubbard" is a name we all know; it is fairly common. But "Kin"? For years, knowing him, I puzzled myself about why that was his name. I kept wondering why he had chosen it and from what he had abbreviated it. And then it came to me that he had not purposely done it. It just happened on him. At any rate, he awoke one morning and found that one touch of nature had indeed made the whole world Kin's.

Booth Tarkington

THE FIRST ALMANACK

BY MISS GERM WILLIAMS

The first almanack printed in Europe was probably the Kalendarium Novum and was gotten up by a chap named Regiomontanus. It was published at Buda, Hungary. It sold readily for ten crowns of gold, the publisher getting nine crowns and a half out of a possible ten. This was in 1475, so it will be seen that even at that early period the impression prevailed among publishers that an author cared little or nothing for money.

January

Black Janiveer starts the world off anew,
Good resolutions and breakovers, too.

January 14, 1879. Isaac Moon, prominent argiculturalist, died near Dayton, Ohio. His cultivator may still be seen standing in the open field just where he left it six months before he died.

To Exterminate Roaches

Procure a box of roach powder from the nearest drug store, being careful to have the druggist guarantee it. Scatter the powder freely in the crevices about the sink and pantry, repeating the dose each day until the powder is all gone. In a few days the roaches will arrive at the conclusion that you are not going to buy any more and will desert the premises.

Born—To Mr. and Mrs. Ike Sanders, Jonesville, Idaho, a child, January 10, 1907.

Next t' a circus ther hain't nothin' that packs up an' tears out any quicker'n th' Christmas spirit.

Miss Fawn Lippincut's cousin, o' Canal Dover, Ohio, is visitin' her. He looks a good deal like a feller that'd go up on th' stage if a magician invited him.

In using a carpet-sweeper with one hand and carrying the baby with the other it will be found very difficult to reach a hair-pin back of the piano.

Enlisting in the United States navy to see the world is like going to the workhouse to learn broommaking.

Uncle Ez Pash has voted th' Dimmycratic ticket free o' charge all his life.

Kentucky has poor feud laws.

A feller don't have over two er three real friends in a lifetime. Once in a while you meet some one that's nice an' clever, but he generally turns out t' be an agent fer somethin'.

When two homely people meet they allus seem glad t' see each other.

RELATION OF THE TURNIP TO EARLY
JOURNALISM IN INDIANA

BY HON. EX-EDITOR CALE FLUHART

The turnip played no unimportant part in the establishment of the newspaper in Indiana. . . . It was no uncommon thing for a sturdy backwoodsman or a thrifty squaw to enter my editorial sanctum jingling their turnips and leaving their names for a year's subscription. . . .

It was no easy task in those days to print a paper that pleased the Indians. . . . An Indian lady belonging to a prominent Mac-o-Chee family once publicly cow-hided me for failing to include her among a number of successful contestants at a scalping party. . . .

The early Indiana editor manufactured his own type rollers, using a combination of New Orleans sorghum and glue. . . .

The type rollers were made many thousands of feet under ground, and great precaution was taken to prevent the fumes of the boiling sorghum from penetrating the forest fastness. It was a process which called for much bravery and hardship.

The mechanical devices for printing a newspaper in the early twenties were primitive indeed. Once when my press broke down I had to wait almost two years for repairs to be brought across the mountains on pack mules. When overtaken by such catastrophes it was my rule to print the paper on a cider press, using a thick, black butter made from wild crab apples for ink. . . .

One dark night in 1828, I was sitting in my sanctum counting turnips, when my attention was called to a light tap on the door. Suddenly it opened and I found myself looking into the bright razor-edged muzzle of a tomahawk held above the head of a tall, raw-boned, smooth-shaven Cherokee Indian. His eyes flashed fire and a strong odor of slumgullion hovered about him. He at once took a copy of last week's paper and pointed to a news item about an affair that had happened at West Liberty, Ohio, four years before. With great presence of mind I coldly reached for my editorial scissors and carefully clipped the article referred to and threw it into the waste basket. This pleased him mightily and he left turnips enough for two years' subscription and even ordered the paper sent regularly to a sister living in Iowa.

February

Bleak February, dreary and gray,
If it be Leap Year, has a twenty-ninth day.

WEATHER NOTES FOR FEBRUARY

February comes in like a big, husky country girl with a tinge of red on her cheek that looks as though it might have been placed there with a stencil. Sometimes she seems to shrink, and other times she seems to push forward as if followed by a traveling salesman.

GROUND HOG DAY

In this country the second day of February is called Ground Hog Day. On this date the little animal peeps out of his home on the hillside after his long winter's sleep. If the weather is dark and threatening he emerges and walks around his home premises and gets ready for the spring rush—the farmer taking this activity as a sign of warm weather; if the day is bright and sunshiny the ground hog quickly retires at the first sight of his shadow. This the farmer thinks, is an unmistakable sign of six more weeks of winter weather and he returns to his checker board.

Th' hardest thing is t' take less when you kin git more.

Women allus brag about th' very things ther husbands keep still about.

It's allus dangerous t' call on a amateur.

A widow an' her money are soon spotted.

If th' Gover'ment wuz as afraid o' disturbin' th' consumer as it is o' disturbin' business, this would be some democracy.

Burglars carried off Miss Tawney Apple's furs last night, an' bloodhounds traced 'em as fer as th' livery stable when they became confused.

Who remembers th' ole-time short-change circus grafter that said, "Five an' ten are thirty an' ten is a dollar, I thank you"?

Th' feller that belittles his wife in company is only tryin' t' pull her down t' his own size.

Some folks have a way o' doin' nothin' that kin hardly be distinguished from work.

Th' feller who raises a garden, like th' feller who marries fer money, never figures in his labor.

Some folks are like a skyrocket. They make a noisy git away, burst an' are never heard of agin.

PSYCHIC PHENOMENA

Dream lore is placed under the head of psychic phenomena. The student of present-day psychology and other scientific people are not inclined to give much thought to the varied influences of dreams, yet many instances are shown of prophetic warnings which seem almost incredible.

In a fearful dream two weeks ago, Miss Cyril Jones, whose grandfather is 117 years old, was foretold that he could not live much longer. To-day he is confined to his room.—Springfield, Ill., *Despatch.*

To dream of rhubarb denotes that you are of a jovial nature and will stand for most anything. To dream of eating it means that you are failing mentally.

To dream of seeing turkeys with plug hats on playing lawn tennis is a sign you will have to cut your booze out.

EX-EDITOR CALE FLUHART

"I am dumfounded at the preposterous arguments sometimes offered by our friends of the gold standard, and it seems to me that it will be many decades before our country recovers its equilibrium after the greatest of all national disgraces, the silver crime of seventy-three. The workings of the gold standard can no better be illustrated than by the fact that if you toss a five-dollar gold piece into a crowd one man gets it. If you fling five silver dollars into the same throng five men

get them, thus proving conclusively a vicious and discriminating system of distribution under the gold standard."
—Extract from the famous speech of Ex-Editor Cale Fluhart, delivered at Roundhead, Ohio, before the Society for the Suppression of Blind Accordion Players.

A BAD OMEN
It is a bad omen to get mixed up in a
stuffy jam with a stout lady wearing goat furs.

1852—Harriet Beecher Stowe writes Uncle Tom's Cabin, little dreaming that it would be the stepping-stone to the stage for 20,000 blonde children.

March

Old windy March, first month of Spring
Flat dwellers grow restless and janitors sing.

Constant Reader, Lilac, Indianny—Th' little poem by Miss Fawn Lippincut, which you asked fer, is printed herewith:—

Oh, th' purty little birds!
How I love t' hear them sing,
Ez they flit from tree t' tree—
Let me count them, one, two, three!
Some er red an' some er blue,
But th' red er very few.

Prof. Harner

Prof. Clem Harner is the sole instigator of the Brown County Silver Cornet Band, which plays on the slightest pretense. Two decades ago Prof. Harner was identified with a number of travelling caravans and talks in the most captivating and intelligent manner about being overcome by canned tomatoes at Tombstone, Arizona, and of once spending a whole afternoon between trains at Urbana, Ohio. Professor Harner has also shaken hands with William Jennings Bryan twenty-two times and narrowly averted hearing Hon. Charles Warren Fairbanks speak at Shoals, Indiana two years ago.

During the last campaign Professor Harner and his associate players serenaded Hon. J. Ham Lewis at a hotel at Paris, Indiana. On this occasion Mr. Lewis appeared on the balcony in pearl-colored silk pajamas and told them a negro dialect story that they had only heard eight times.

Lafe Bud

Lafe Bud developed a hatred for agriculture early in life and began a commercial career by taking up with a crayon portrait house and preying on the humbler classes. He can now ride with the window down, registers from New York and can look at a bill o' fare without being seized with indecision. Mr. Bud is in his twenty-eighth year and has been married five times and still carries a cane and a pocketful of lavender buds. He has been blackballed out of two suit clubs and lost his first travelling position for charging five dollars for supper at Kokomo in his expense account.

THE AMATEUR ACTOR

BY TELL BINKLEY

An amateur actor is a fellow who can not act. He is ready and willing to act, and often looks like he could act, but he can not.

Every town supports at least one amateur actor. It has to, for after the amateur actor gets a whiff of the footlights and a complimentary puff in the home weekly he at once becomes disqualified for further usefulness and loafs from one local entertainment to the next.

In appearance an amateur actor does not differ materially from a high school teacher or a saddler. Occasionally there is one with an ashen pallor and black curly hair and eyes like a locomotive engineer who has washed up hurriedly after a long, smoky run. But the average amateur actor would not cause more than passing notice should he be seen leaning on the town pump or stepping into the postoffice.

It doesn't make a particle of difference to an amateur actor what play is up for rehearsal. He is long on memorizing, and "Don Caesar," "William Tell," "The Naiad Queen" or "The Pirates of Penzance" all look alike to him. He can sing a ballad, or will sing one whether he can or not, and jump at the chance to do a Highland fling. The only time he ever has stage fright is when the theater threatens to burn the day before he expects to "act.". . . Nothing pleases an amateur actor quite so much as to have someone ask him why he never adopted the stage as a profession. If his mother is alive it's because she wants him at home. But if she is dead he will assume a serious air and say, "Aw, it's a dog's life."

SOME FACTS ABOUT THE MOON

The moon's motion on her axis, unlike the electric-light plant in a small town, is entirely uniform. Her angular velocity in her orbit, like a vaudeville program, is subject to slight change. The moon's surface contains about 14,685,000 square miles of good brick land, but no atmosphere and no water. A profound silence reigns over the desolate clay surface sustaining the old theory that no women abide there. A great many people plant garden seeds by the moon, and, in some instances, farmers have plowed by the moon in order to get off the following day to attend the circus. Crocheting by moonlight is extremely injurious to the eyes. There will be an eclipse of the moon at Shelbyville, Ind., May 10, 1908.

HINTS TO FARMERS

After a farmer's wife cuts his hair she should always scald the crock before putting it back in the milk-house.

If you have buggy harness, use insect powder.

April

Uncertain April, sunshine and showers,
Soggy wet stockings and faded silk flowers.

Next t' fallin' o'er a wheelbarrow in th' dark ther haint nothin' a feller likes better'n hearin' his wife tell about somethin' cute he did while sparkin'.

You're never successful till you're happy.

Th' feller that's satisfied is gittin' ole.

It's a wise father that knows his own daughter.

Anybuddy that's too nice t' eat cornbread is too nice fer a democracy.

Politics makes strange goodfellers.

A Windsor tie'll be found very effective in hidin' a fluctuatin' Adam's apple.

Ever' once in a while we meet a feller that's too proud t' beg, an' too honest t' steal, an' too lazy t' work.

Th' feller that says "I may be wrong, but—" does not believe ther kin be any such possibility.

Nothin's as mean as givin' a little child somethin' useful fer Christmas.

It hain't a bad plan t' keep still occasionally even when you know what you're talkin' about.

The General Store

Mat Thompson's general store had been sort o' a continuous Chatalky er clearin' house fer political debaters, students o' international affairs an' general all 'round gossips fer many years. . . . His store wuz an emporium where you could git most anything from beeswax t' wind mills. Th' rusty brackets, er lamp holders, that hung from th' ceilin' wuz festooned with fly specked dried apples that wuz strung on a cord after th' fashion o' beads. Th' gents' furnishin's, cheviot shirts, paper collars an' overalls, wuz kept in barrels an' th' showcases wuz full o' onions an' axle grease. Mat only sold one brand o' se-gars, th' 'Cock Robin.' It wuz a black, hard, flinty, arrow shaped, prison made twofer that pulled on th' bit an' went out on th' least sign o' inattention er neglect. Mat used t' say that he jist kept 'em 'cause you couldn't talk so much if you smoked 'em. . . .

VELMA'S VOW

BY MISS FAWN LIPPINCUT

To the Reader

There is a popular belief that novel writing is very difficult. It is not. Very few problems come up during the writing of a novel that cannot be readily mastered. There are certain things about trees and flowers which have to be looked up, and there are peculiarities about certain sections of our country (and perhaps other countries) that one should have a general knowledge of in order to be a strong, forceful novelist. Some very excellent novels are ruined through too little attention being given to seemingly trivial things. The same may be said of plays. I have in mind a certain play in particular wherein a character in a very effective scene is made to say, "Ah, nature has been teaching us a lesson. See, a pretty meadow lark has built her nest in the mouth of this rusty cannon!" As a matter of fact, a meadow lark was never known to build its nest anywhere except flat on the ground. In "Velma's Vow" I have tried to have everything blooming at the right time, and I am sure that none of the stirring situations which show the trials and tribulations which beset my heroine at evey turn in her path to happiness is overdrawn. Indeed life itself is too melodramatic to need any embellishment from us novel writers. I have penned this simple

FAWN LIPPINCUT

tale, dear reader, with the hope that it will be the means of bringing many to realize that riches and grand surroundings are no match for fate, and that only the truest love can batter down the forces that all too often obstruct the road to real happiness.

Miss Fawn Lippincut.

APRIL 19 TO MAY 20

SIGN OF TAURUS (THE BULL)

The Romans dedicated the month of April to the bright planet, Venus, holding the twenty-third day sacred to her honor. People born between the dates of April 19 and May 20, inclusive, enter life under the guidance of Taurus, a strong, husky sign bequeathing to its proteges all the sterling attributes a newspaper hands to a prominent citizen after he is dead—if he has been a subscriber.

These people are the squatty, snarled apple-trees of society. They assume Life's heritage at a time when Tennessee strawberries and long, bright green, tasteless cucumbers invade the markets, and Nature, tired of her mantle of snow and ice, warms up to the situation. The heirs of Taurus have self-reliance and buoyancy of spirit, and frequently reach high places—such positions as postmaster and constable. They are seldom talkative and are fond of canned corn. Especially is this true of the men who marry Taurus women, for it matters not how much money he owes, you can never tell it by looking at his wife. As long as he can get credit, her faithful feet will follow. Hers is the devotion of Clytie, who lived just out of Upper Sandusky, Ohio, and became enamored of Helios, a pianola salesman of good address, and followed him to Niles, Ohio, where he died as he had lived—a profligate.

Taurus people inherit an excellent physique that endures many years. A well-known and popular Taurus woman is to-day traveling with a burlesque company, posing in *Rock of Ages* at the age of 79. When Fate directs them toward Italy, Sicily, Northern Spain or Louisville, Kentucky, they lose their buoyancy.

May

Bright smiling May, pink rhubarb and greens,
We long for the forests, meadows and streams.

May, 1898—Admiral George Dewey, U.S.A., blew a few old disabled Spanish hulks out of Manila Bay, awakening the officers and men and scattering them in the surf. Little or nothing is ever heard of Dewey these days.

A worm won't turn if you know how t' step on it.

We kin beat our muskets an' swords int' plowshares, but who's goin' t' beat our boys int' plowin?

It seems like next t' a bull terrier nothin' holds on like a feller with a wet hand.

"I allus go t' th' circus in th' forenoon while th' hippopotamus is awake," said Mrs. Min Nugent, t'day.

Of all th' substitutes a substitute speaker is th' worst.

It's th' feller that works when ther's nothin' t' do that gits t' th' front.

A small p'tato never gits t' th' top.

Th' feller that gits ahead o' his story wouldn' be so bad if he stayed ahead.

Professor Clem Harner has written a bassoon solo entitled, "Echoes from th' Abatoir."

Stew Nugent has decided t' go t' work till he kin find somethin' better.

When a Dimmycrat gits defeated he says his wife didn' want him t' run; an' when a Republican gits snowed under he says th' people are follerin' strange gods.

HINTS TO FARMERS

In operating a corn shredder a farmer should caution his wife against getting her apron caught in the machinery while he is in town playing pool.

Be very careful about currying favor with a mule.

When drilling for wheat a farmer should see to it that his horses stand erect, keep perfect step and are provided with both right and left flanks.

There is nothing much to be said in favor of late plowing. Eminent authorities say that under no circumstances should a farmer plow later than 10 o'clock. It keeps the horses up late and the dew rusts the plow.

Take a nickel's worth o' rhubarb an' add five dollars' worth o' sugar an' cook till done an' you've got one o' th' most expensive liver regulators on th' market.

Kate Bender

In th' early seventies ther wuz a family named Bender that lived in a lonely spot in Labette County, Kansas, and there they earned a decent living, but not by agriculture, or even cattle raisin'. Th' Bender cabin lay along side o' th' ole Sante Fe trail t' Californy. T' th' weary traveler this cabin loomed up like th' Woolworth buildin' agin th' western horizon as he trudged along in th' soft light o' th' closin' day. Th' pride o' th' Bender family wuz a big Clydesdale daughter named Kate. She had a low, scowlin' brow, wide, brown feet an' a thick massive chin. She had th' stealth an' cunnin' of a panther, an' could sniff a victim many

"KATE"

hours before he knocked on th' Bender door fer food an' shelter. Seated before th' hearth fire's ruddy glow th' stranger would impart th' latest news o' th' Greeley campaign an' other gossip back in th' states, while Kate rolled up her sleeves an' grabbed her dogwood maul an' caved in his bean from behind. Long before th' cock's first salutation t' th' morn, th' stranger, stripped o' even th' gold in his teeth, lay buried beneath th' wide spreadin' boughs o' a cottonwood tree in th' back yard. Kate made a nice livin' fer her aged father an' mother, t' both o' whom she wuz strongly attached. After they died she went straight, an' died this side o' Boone, Iowa.

QUESTIONS AND ANSWERS

CONDUCTED BY DR. MOPPS

I am often kidded about my slender arms. How can I develop them?—Elcie.

ANSWER—Scrubbing is a splendid remedy. Get down on your knees and scrub first with one hand and then with the other for eight hours each day, letting your full weight rest on the thumb and forefinger of either hand.

Is there no simple home preparation that will make my hands soft and pretty?—Lucile.

ANSWER—One cupful of milk, one cupful of cornmeal, one cupful of sugar. Put the baking powder in the last thing.

Papa is thinking some of breaking up and losing everything. Kindly suggest some honorable employment for a sensible young lady of eighteen.—Mildred.

ANSWER—General housework is the least worked field.

Can you inform me of anything cheaper than Sunday newspapers for fuel?—Myrtle.

ANSWER—Breakfast food samples.

Miss Pet Plum will enter th' beauty contest bein' conducted by th' Roundhead, Ohio, *Bugle-Gazette*. Miss Plum is a dark bay, an' th' poet might say—

> Her head is like the th' Autumn wind—
> She has th' winsome peacock's eye.

Her complexion is dark pink like th' true mother o' pearl, changin' like a chameleon with her varyin' moods. She has an alkali nose an' a dimple on her chin caused by fallin' on a stump when a child. Her head is crowned by a mass o' superb hair—now dark brown, now yaller, jist as she takes a notion. Miss Plum is six feet two an' weighs eighty-five pounds an' has a beautiful willowy carriage.

1899—The South African War began, the Boers fighting behind rocks and the English fighting behind the Irish.

June

Warm, leafy June and perspiring young brides,
Grooms that are worthy and grooms that are snides.

It takes adversity t' produce a first class human being.

Every girl should have two fellers, one she likes an' one who spends his money freely.

Th' feller thet kin quote anythin' hesn't necessarily got any more sense than a parrot.

Some fellers are like a hen, fer ther allus gittin' credit fer somethin' they couldn' help doin'.

Who remembers when women used t' step out o' ther skirts instead o' squirm out o' them?

Some folks hate t' see a feller succeed, even if he's workin' fer th' Lord.

Th' only thing that carries more baggage than a opery company is a woman travelin' with two babies.

It seems like it takes an unusually smart feller t' git by with a good education.

Jealousy is as hard t' hide as a bass drum.

A good many people are like ortomobiles—the cheaper they are the more noise they make.

THE HOME-COMING OF BROUGH McGEE

BY MISS GERM WILLIAMS

It has been many a year since any public event brought to the surface as much lively interest as the home coming exercises at Melodeon Hall last Thursday night in honor of Mr. Brough McGee. Every available inch of space was utilized, and many late comers had to either return home or hang around and play pool at the Little Gem. Professor Clem Harner's silver cornet band played "Home, Sweet Home," and was immediately followed by Mr. Alex Tansey, who delivered the address of welcome without referring to his notes once. It was most brilliant, instructive and eloquent, and to those who know Mr. Tansey only casually it was indeed a great surprise. His knowledge of life and conditions on

MR. BROUGH McGEE

the plains in the early days shows much studiousness. Mr. Tansey spoke in full as follows:

"Ladies, Gentlemen of the Band, and Gentlemen—There has been in my life, though brief as it has been, so to speak, two particularly bright epochs, so to speak, that stand out on memory's scroll like two great golden teeth in the face of time, as I might say in way of illustration, so to speak. The first was my privilege in introducing William Jennings Bryan to the citizens of Shoals, Indiana. The second, the distinguished honor of having been chosen . . . to introduce to you one who, though distinguished in no lesser degree, though along widely different lines, so to speak, is thereby no less distinguished. (Liberal applause.) Our subject this evening is a man, who, in the prime of young manhood, good and manly, struck out westward at a time when men were tried as at no other time in our country's time. (Applause.) A time when the westward traveler, so to speak, encountered in his pathway innumerable dangers without number. Where the unbroken trail to the then great unknown, so to speak, passed through a labyrinth of peril, pathos and pestilence. Danger lurked behind each nodding cacti and scrubby sage brush. . . . On and on, and on again, he trudged over jagged peaks, through gloomy, echoful canyons, always within hailing distance of hostile savages, though being careful not to hail. . . . So, I say, it is a great honor to stand here tonight before this great audience and splendid band, by universal request, and have the distinguished honor, so to speak, to introduce to you a man who, though ripe in years and whose career is crowned with success, comes back to you the same genial nature's nobleman. My friends and band, I have the distinguished pleasure of introducing to you Mr. Brough McGee, of Apache County, Nevada."

As Mr. Tansey took his seat amid wild cheering, Mr. McGee arose dressed in a tight fitting brown and black suit and spoke in thick, blunt tones in full as follows:

"I hain't no speech maker. I like to hear 'em, but I don't make 'em. I guess nobuddy here remembers me. You wuz all little shavers when I went West in the fifties 'bout the time the Haines boys killed their mother. It took a lot o' grit to go West them days. I done pretty well I guess, but I had to have grit. If you hain't got grit in the West they'll eat you up."

At the conclusion of Mr. McGee's address a number of our older citizens hung about him while the crowd was moving out.

JUNE 21 TO JULY 22

SIGN OF CANCER (THE CRAB)

After a stormy debate lasting some days, the Romans decided to dedicate the radiant month of June to Luna, the moon-eyed goddess. Persons ushered into this vale of tears during the latter half of this fickle month, or along about the Fourth of July, enter life under doubtful influences, and are liable to be cancer specialists. Though gifted in many directions to the brink of genius, they are described by Emerson as "always looking for money from home." Being neither broad-minded nor open to conviction, nothing will shake their belief that the foreigner pays the tax. Domestic in their nature, they long for the close companionship of home life, and will often stick there till they are forty or forty-five years old without paying any board. They occasionally pursue harmonious, conventional ways of life, but seldom vote the Democratic ticket.

July

Sultry July with her great celebrations,
Firecrackers, music and young lawyers' orations.

By common consent all over the northern hemisphere, July is allowed to be the hottest month of all the year.

July 17, 1820. Harold LeClair, actor, was born at Bucksport, Maine. LeClair first discovered that tomatoes were edible while essaying the part of Hamlet at Ann Arbor, Michigan.

The day following the third day of this month is known as the Fourth of July in this country. It is the anniversary of the Declaration of Independence, which occurred on that date in 1776. Since that time it has been customary to celebrate the occasion throughout the United States. A salute is fired at sunrise, noon and evening from every fort, man-o'-war and courthouse yard in America on this day. In towns without courthouses it is fired anyway.

In communities where the saloon keepers and restaurant proprietors get together and work harmoniously the celebration is always a success. The band gets out and plays and the boys, decked out in their flashy uniforms, receive many a shy glance from the starched belles of the village and vicinity; the hook and ladder company makes a spurt or two up and down Main street and stacks on the public square while some member, clad in home-made "tights," climbs the ladder with all the agility of a squirrel. The greased pole contest is easily the most enjoyable event on the program and the crowd fairly takes on a purple hue from convulsive outbursts of laughter.

The speaker's stand is located exactly in the center of town in order that all of the storekeepers will have an equal chance. It is draped with cheap bunting and a picture of George Washington. The orator of the day is generally a young and struggling lawyer who had spoken for the honor months ahead—or at the time the saloon men first thought of having a celebration. He is arrayed in a glossy, tight-fitting Prince Albert and a white lawn tie, and when he rises to speak he shines like a trained seal. A number of early residents occupy seats on the stand and add materially to the tone and dignity of things. After trying to swallow a drink of water and nervously arranging his manuscript the orator opens up with a brief review of our country's progress, being careful not to mix in any politics. By the time his collar wilts and sinks out of sight he tackles the "Declaration," and the people walk away in twos and threes.

At eight p.m. sharp, the destruction of "$10,000 worth of fireworks," at a cost of $12.00, begins from the roof of the People's Bank, and the jollifying continues till the last Roman candle has been dodged and nobody is left but the "night constable."

A NEWSPAPER EDITOR

Th' feller that stands up on th' nineteenth story o' a steel frame in January an' ketches red hot rivets in his apron is a loafer compared t' th' editur o' a newspaper. . . . A editur must be a great diplomat. He must be evasive and direct; he must understand th' manly art o' self defense an' talk entertain'ly about the complicated condition o' European affairs. . . . He should wear glasses on a cord an' have a pale forehead an' above all he should have an unyieldin' spine an' th' courage t' say "Yes."

Ex-Editor Cale Fluhart

August

August and ragweeds, hay fever takes hold,
If you can't jingle money, you've just got a cold.

August is the car shortage month, and the merry songs of the harvest hands, as they drive out of town loaded down with jugs and plug tobacco, harmonize roughly with the peace and quiet of the lazy summer afternoon. It was believed by the Romans that the pre-eminent warmth of August had something to do with the rising and setting of the star Canicula—the Little Dog, therefore they conferred the name of Dog Days on the first eleven days of the month.

Ever'buddy's on a vacation an' th' ole town is as
quiet as a prominent woman's husband.

Miss Tawney Apple, who is t' be married in September,
has asked fer a respite.

At eight o'clock, Friday morning, August third, 1492, Christopher Columbus pushed away from the public landing at Palos, Spain, and later discovered America.

August sixth, 1623, Shakespeare's wife died; on the same date in 1848, a sea serpent was sighted off the Cape of Good Hope.

Some time during the month of August, 1593, Isaac Walton, the patron saint of fishermen, was born at Stafford, England.

August, 1794, the Duke of Sussex had his marriage annulled.

August fifteenth, 1738, Joe Miller, an actor and wit, passed to the dark beyond at St. Clement Dane's parish.

August, 1778, the Duke of Devonshire stopped the famous Festival of Tutbury after the police had allowed it to run unmolested for four hundred years.

T' err is human, but t' admit it haint.

Popularity should begin at home.

AUGUST 22 TO SEPTEMBER 22

SIGN OF VIRGO (THE VIRGIN)

August, the month when Kansas yells for help, was dedicated to Ceres, goddess of corn, by the oldtimers.

Folks born the latter half of this month or the first two weeks of September belong to the dry food class, and enter upon the stage of life under the sign of Virgo, indicating an inborn aptitude to voice the mind of the public before the public is really aware of the issues. Virgo heirs make great newspaper reporters. Their manner of digging up news is so engaging that their informant does not wake up until the paper has gone to press and the reporter is well on his way to the golf links, chuckling all the while. A Virgo reporter always carries an old sleeve to laugh in. Excellent as this investigative turn of mind may be, the proteges of Virgo often get their newspapers in a jam on account of their unconquerable mania for getting all the news, and their editors have to go home in closed carriages for weeks at a time.

September

September, the month of the old country fair,
"One more an' we'll start" is heard here and there.

September twenty, 1815, William Hutton, the Birmingham, England, publisher, was born. Biography records scarcely a finer instance of industry and economy leading their possessor out of the most unpropitious circumstances to honor and affluence. Hutton's father was a man who could drink or leave it alone, so William was early set to work, walking fourteen miles to his task and carrying his dinner, which consisted of a cold buckwheat cake.

A young wife's biscuits make a dandy border fer a geranium bed.

There is nothing so aggravating as a fresh boy that is too old to ignore or too young to kick.

"It's hard enough t' git somethin' fer somethin', t' say nothin' o' somethin' fer nothin'," said Lafe Bud t'day, as he threw a circular letter away.

Miss Fawn Lippincut says her objection to a tourin' car is that you can't throw th' lines around th' whip.

NEW MELODEON HALL

During the closed season for theatricals Melodeon Hall has undergone many notable changes. The walls about the ticket office window have been handsomely whitewashed and the railing along the gallery stairway has been neatly sandpapered. It is the intention of Constable Newt Plum, who has assumed the management of the popular old playhouse, to make other important changes. If his present plans carry, an effort will be made to oust Tell Binkley, who occupies a lower floor room just in the rear of the livery stable end. If this can be brought about a dressing room will be added, thus making the theater one of the most comfortable as well as the most modern opera halls west of Lima, Ohio. Manager Plum is also determined to put an end to the old custom, so long popular with the patrons of the theater, of eating sardines during a performance and throwing the empty boxes on the floor and elsewhere.

THE POPULAR OLD PLAYOUSE

It hain't no trouble fer a feller with a good reputation an' a wide circle o' friends t' steal all th' money he wants if he's built that way.

It often happens that a feller's usefulness ends when his salary is raised.

Constable Newt Plum accidentally locked his whiskers up in a cash register last night an' it wuz three o'clock before his cries fer help wuz heard.

A slangy evangelist does about as much good as an auctioneer.

Venus will be Morning Star till September 14; then Evening Star the rest of the year.
Jupiter will be Evening Star till July 16; then Morning Star the rest of the year. Subject to change.

Miss Germ Williams

Miss Germ Williams first attracted public attention through her brilliant editorials in various poultry journals and her many valuable suggestions pertaining to farm life in America are eagerly sought and relished by people of all professions. She is the real type of the literary woman, paying little attention to her hair or the commonest rules of tidiness. She is inclined to bulkiness and straight lines and would not let a social obligation stand in the way of an onion in a thousand years. Following are a few choice selections from Miss William's pen:

A farmer will find patent leather shoes to be more comfortable if, before putting them on, he breaks an egg in each one. Any kind of eggs will answer.

In a country home where spaghetti is quite popular whiskers should either be abandoned entirely or closely trimmed about the mouth. Any kind of scissors will do.

Emerson's Essays and Plutarch's Lives may now be had in cheap but durably bound editions. Why not make the farm attractive?

In addition to her earnings from poultry and dairy products a farmer's wife may add a snug sum to her exchequer by the cultivation of camels. The combings of these useful animals are made into brushes of the finest texture and are much in demand.

THE STAGE

*Some Notable Players Who Have Trod the Melodeon
Hall Boards During the Current Season.*

BY MISS GERM WILLIAMS

MISS HATTIE LECLAIR

No actress in our time has ever leaped into popular favor with the agility of Hattie LeClair. Our theater-goers will remember her great naturalness and poise with ever increasing fondness. As Myrtle, in "Marion Gray or the Lost Heiress of Red Stone Hall" she grasped every requirement with determination and grace. It was my privilege during her engagement among us to sit directly behind two grocery salesmen from Dayton, Ohio, and it was, indeed, a pleasure to note the effect Miss LeClair's acting had on them. . . . They fairly raved over her acting only going out once between acts. The climax of their excitement came during the scene in the fourth act between Myrtle and Jack Carrington, the young squire, when she spurns him in no uncertain terms, saying as she tossed his ring into the grass, "Sir, I would rather be a poor sewing machine girl all my life than accept a favor from you!" When Carrington struck his boot with his riding whip and started to strangle her, the two Dayton salesmen grabbed their hats and rushed up the center aisle for the stage door, vowing vengeance on the cowardly brute.

During Miss Le Clair's brief stay in our midst she hurriedly ran through the manuscript of Mr. Alex Tansey's play, "The Slaves of Catarrh," and pronounced it full of splendid possibilities.

October

Then comes October, mellow and brown
Farmer and pumpkins start early for town.

Nothin' fades like popularity if it's overexposed.

Th' more important a feller gits around a concern th' easier it seems t' git along while he is on a vacation.

Tilford Moots got a letter from a newspaper sayin' his time wuz up an' t'day he wrote his will.

Speakin' o' th' high cost o' courtin', who remembers when all a feller needed wuz a narrow buggy an' a sack o' red cinnamon drops?

Miss Mazie Bud is gittin' t' be so purty she haint got a girl friend.

Next t' an exemplary citizen nobuddy gits as lonesome as a retired farmer.

No husband is ever so ugly that his wife don't pretend t' be jealous o' him.

How sadly we're reminded o' th' fleetin' years when we git out an' try t' fly a kite fer th' children.

JOINERS

Th' funeral o' Gabe Petty, who died Thursday, wuz th' largest ever held in th' county. Mr. Petty belonged t' ever'thing in town an' owed ever'buddy in th' county. It wuz his purpose had he lived t' run fer sheriff next spring. Th' foregoin' should make us pause. That ther's entirely too much joinin' an' organizin' goin' on in this age ther kin be no doubt. It's gittin' so ever' community, from th' interurban stop with its platform an' milk cans t' th' ordorus city, is split up an' divided off int' cliques an' clubs an' societies an' cheap insurance lodges. It's gittin' so th' first thing three or four people

MR. GABE PETTY

do after they git chummy is t' organize. Ever'buddy you meet these days is backed up by a half a dozen different clubs an' lodges. If they git sick ther looked after; if they git in trouble, ther defended; if they loaf, ther fed, if they work ther paid more than they earn, an' if they run fer office, ther generally elected. Ther's too many people tryin' t' help 'emselves by belongin' t' somethin' instead o' gittin' out an' hustlin'—entirely too many mediocre people tryin' t' boost 'emselves both politically, socially an' financially by joinin' ever'thing in sight. Oh fer th' ole days when ever' tub stood on its own bottom an' folks were known by what they were an' not by what they belonged to.
—From th' *Bloom Center Weekly Slip Horn*

SIDELIGHTS ON THE CHARACTERS OF THOSE WHO HAVE SUCCEEDED

BY EDITOR CALE FLUHART

A series of highly interesting and illuminating biographies from the gifted pen of Cale Fluhart, who at the age of eighty-five, has returned to journalism and assumed the editorial mantle of the *Bloom Center Weekly Sliphorn*. In these personal glimpses the veteran editor reveals much that has hitherto been undreamed of concerning the lives of such notable people as Wes Whipple, Schuyler Wiggins, Alex Newton, Curly Prince, Miss Bonnie Grimes, Teckla Bramble, Wilbur Green, Abigail Ainsley, Barton Crosby, Elmer Titus, Judge Warren Berry, Benton Swallow, Lester Slocum and others.

MISS BONNIE GRIMES

Early durin' th' reconstruction period follerin' th' dreadful civil war, Miss Bonnie Grimes, nee Mrs. Art Ball, wuz born in th' classic river town of Aurora, Indianny, noted fer its perpendicular door yards an' casket factory. While still in arms, her parents moved t' Bloom Center with th' Model Stave Works, where she received a good plain education an' blossomed int' th' belle o' th' town. One mild May afternoon after walkin' by th' Central House four or five times, she met Mr. Art Ball, a drummer glib o' tongue an' o' preposessin' appear-

ance. When evenin' come an' she did not appear fer supper as she wuz want t' do, her mother supposed that she wuz bein' held by an extra innin' o' croquet game an' went ahead with th' dishes as usual. Toward midnight word wuz received from th' livery stable that she had eloped with a dashin' stranger. Later a telegram from Lawrenceburg announced her marriage. Arrivin' home shortly thereafter she became a great help t' her mother an' rarely ventured forth. In th' course of a year she established th' Locust Hill Poultry Farm, featurin' th' celebrated Black Minorcas. By close application t' business Miss Bonnie soon became a power in th' poultry world an' a valued contributor t' many publications devoted t' th' hen. From th' bell o' th' countryside t' th' serious minded, evenly poised an' thorough goin' queen o' th' hennery, her transfermation has been complete. Bereft o' romance, fashion an' empty twaddle, she is t'day a useful woman in a practical age, fully demonstratin' t' th' world what her sex is capable of when removed from th' cowerin', domineerin' influence o' man.

"CURLY" PRINCE

"Curly" Prince! What a flood of memories that name will awaken among our older citizens. Dashin', intrepid, debonair Bob Prince, or "Curly" Prince, as he wuz affectionately known almost two generations ago, wuz th' only an' idolized child o' Hiram an' Amanda Prince, who settled in Bloom Center in th' fifties. Rich an' indulgent, Bob Prince's parents gratified his ever' whim. He wuz given th' refusal of all th' best colleges, an' his extensive wardrobe comprised, besides all th' nobby creations o' th' period, an assortment o' fancy waistcoats that wuz th' envy of all th' pool rooms. A wizard among th' girls, a lover o' athletics an' cologne, a genius with th' cue an' th' personification o' grace itself on th' ball room floor, "Curly" seemed t' have ever'thing but an education an' a trade. Many will recall his faultless alligator shoes an' bell bottomed trousers, his glistenin' tile an' silken mustache, his low chiseled forehead an' wealth o' raven curls. Ever' notable function wuz perfumed by his presence, an' gloom overhung ever' social occasion where he failed t' show up. One day his father went on th' note of a friend an' shortly after th' family moved away leavin' a void in th' social life of th' community that never quite healed. Only recently a friend o' th' editur's returned from a trip t' th' northwest an' reported a most joyous five minutes spent with Bob Prince. Handicapped in his early life by wealth, curls an' a love fer athletics, Bob Prince lived t' learn th' seriousness o' life an' t' triumph o'er his early environment. T'day he is a capable an' trusted freight handler in Minneapolis, an' makes a dollar an' seventy cents per day when not strikin'.

MR. TECKLA BRAMBLE

Mr. Teckla Bramble wuz born in th' sixties on th' ole Bramble farm three miles east o' th' pumpin' station an' early gave evidence of a hatred fer agriculture that wuz apparent t' all. After reluctantly follerin' th' plow until his twenty-first year, he sold a calf an' severed all diplomatic relations with his father, an' struck out fer Chicago. After lookin' over th' world an' sizin' up th' opportunities, he hunted up th' city park whose facilities fer deep an' serious reflection are well known t' all who have tried t' gain a foot hold in a crowded an' heartless metropolis. Penniless an' unattached, weak an' stiff from hunger an' exposure, th' world looked black indeed t' Teckla Bramble. Too honorable t' launch forth on a career o' crime an' utterly opposed t' manual labor, he had almost despaired, when, with supernatural strength, he pulled himself t'gether an' decided t' make one more heroic effort t' find somethin' that just suited him. Success crowned his efforts an' he became a street car conductor. Th' clang an' excitement o' his new position seemed t' deaden his finer instincts an' he soon contracted th' wine habit an' later returned t' th' park. It wuz early May an' th' fragrance o' flowers an' th' songs o' birds filled th' air, while umbreller menders, fresh from ther winter sentences, filled the benches an' doped out ther summer itineraries. A new hope filled th' breast o' Teckla Bramble. Could he become an umbreller mender? Others had succeeded, why not he? Th' die wuz cast! Allus close t' nature an' a keen observer, Mr. Bramble's tours have at least been a success educationally, an' t'day he is a veritable storehouse o' anecdote an' information.

The evening of October thirty-one is Hallowe'en or Nut Crack Night. It is clearly a relic of pagan times but is still very popular. It is a night set apart for walking about and playing harmless pranks, such as placing the hotel omnibus on top of the Baptist church or plugging the milkman's pump. On this night, too, young maidens, wishing to know if their sweethearts are on the square or only romancing, try out all sorts of silly tests, such as going to bed with a fried egg in the right hand, or, upon disrobing for the night, to throw their rat over their left shoulder. Should it alight in the powder box, according to superstition the face of their true love will appear in a Peruna ad on the following day.

November

Leafless November, elections galore,
Jubliant candidates and candidates sore.

The first Tuesday after the first Monday in November is an election day of some sort in practically every city and hamlet in the Union.

A slangy evangelist bears about th' same relation t' theology as a bill poster does t' th' theatrical profession.

No stretch o' time'll ever soften th' feelin' agin th' boy who tattled at school.

Ther hain't nothin' as cheap as a good doctor.

Keepin' a marriage a secret must be a good deal like hidin' a bass drum.

Nothin' makes a big, awkward fourteen-year-ole boy as mad as t' have his mother say: "Yes, he's th' baby."

You'd think some folks' names wuz on th' program from th' way they try t' show off in a the-ater.

A good talker is allus a poor listener.

A feller kin have more money than brains an' still be hard up.

Never tell ever'thing t' any one.

Some fellers have a way o' loafin' that makes 'em look busy.

In closely contested rural districts an American election is a beautiful affair. Red-nosed grafters fix up deals in the box stall at the livery stable; stern-visaged inspectors pace to and fro in front of the voting places; excited men with faces flushed with strong drink run in and out of the alleys; repeaters steal along in the shadows of the buildings; long-legged newspaper reporters rush from one precinct to another, eager for any figures that will forecast the result; tottering old men are rushed to the polls in conveyances of every description; clean cut business men walk to their homes on the opposite side of the street; broad shouldered marshals with dyed mustaches and dangerous looking canes stand with their backs to the saloons while the work of electing a clean ticket proceeds.

After the last dollar has been placed in the hand of the independent voter and the last beer keg tipped on end the polls close and the task

of counting up and throwing out proceeds. Early in the evening the populace begins to gather in the criminal court room or the opera hall to hear the returns read aloud. Frequently "grapevines" are freely interspersed, adding much good-natured fun to the pandemonium and causing many really beaten reform candidates to remain up until a late hour.

KEBOBBED OYSTERS

Strangle fifty oysters and singe over an alcohol lamp. Chop enough hay for one truck horse and add a little dash of parsley. Beat two real eggs into insensibility and scatter. Have at easy hailing distance an ordinary baking dish such as magicians use, lift the oysters by the wings and dip them first in the eggs and then in sawdust (in the absence of sawdust bird sand will answer), and throw at once into the baking dish. Cut a table-spoon into small pieces and sprinkle freely over the top and cook in quick oven. Then give them to the man that hauls your ashes.

You can take a voter to th' polls but you can't make him think.

UNCLE NILES TURNER

On the twenty-third day of last November Uncle Niles Turner celebrated his one hundred and third birthday. His faculties are still unimpaired, and he . . . talks interestingly of a very wet spring in the early thirties when every croquet set in the village sprouted.

FORTY YEARS AGO

BY UNCLE NILES TURNER

Th' whole family dressed around th' kitchen stove in th' winter, one at a time.

We all walked home t' dinner at noon.

Nobuddy bought a book if anybuddy in town had th' one he wanted.

A father supported his daughters till they were grown.

Nothin' broke th' monotony o' summer but a one-ring circus.

We called farmers country Jakes.

A feller with a hoss an' phaeton wuz supposed t' be wealthy.

Bacon wuz th' chief diet o' th' poor an' oppressed.

People wore patched shoes.

Nobuddy wuz afraid t' drink at th' town pump.

We used t' borrow a cow t' mow th' lawn.

New shoes squeaked.

Sody fountains closed in September.

We all wore soggy red flannel underwear.

Th' courthouse square wuz a wood market.

Ther wuz a little child swingin' on ever' front gate.

Butchers carried whips that cracked like a gun an' drove ther cattle thro' town.

We only cleaned up on Saturday evenin'.

Nickel cigars had a pleasant odor.

We pressed th' creases out o' ready made pants.

Doctors an' lawyers wore plug hats, often with sack coats.

Hair watch chains an' gold headed canes were plentiful.

Tub oysters set on th' sidewalk by th' hitchin' racks.

Dried apples were strung on a cord.

Kids chewed bees wax.

Ever' bay window wuz full o' geraniums.

Ever' well ordered home had a rockery.

We thought ever' train goin' west wuz goin' t' Californy.

Th' dentists pulled your teeth if they hurt.

Fruit trees looked out fer 'emselves.

Th' best actors that ever lived showed for twenty-five an' fifty cents.

We knew who wrote ever'thing in a newspaper.

Nothin' but saloons an' meat shops took ice.

A woman wouldn' climb in a buggy if anybuddy wuz lookin'.

Ever' doctor carried a saw.

Croquet wuz th' steppin' stone t' th' swellest girl in town.

No overcoat,
No money,
November.

HINTS TO FARMERS

A farmer may cleanse his finger nails
with peroxide of hydrogen with an or-
ange-wood stick and then apply ground
pumice stone to make them look foxy.
Ten times each day is often enough.

Never pick apples with a croquet mallet.

To cure a fresh cow utterly ignore her
and don't laugh at anything she says.

December

Snowy December sweet Christmas time brings
Cheap manicure sets and bright, phoney rings.

With the joyous Christmas season comes a longing that fills the breasts of countless thousands—a longing to be back home again. Even to him who has long been lost to its sweet influences, to the most abject and pitiful wanderer, come visions of a happy childhood, heart-choking recollections of someone near and dear back in the mist of years—an irresistible desire to be back again, somewhere, some place.

What is more beautiful than a Christmas reunion at home where the hand of death has been merciful and the little flock, scattered for years, gathers again under the old roof—mother, father and all the children?

Peace has its victories no less than war, but it doesn't have as many monuments t' unveil.

Hon. Ex-Editor Cale Fluhart lectured on th' "Moral Wave" at Melodeon Hall last night t' a well filled audience.

Th' financial scare has caused so many folks down our way t' bury ther money that th' township looks like a prairie dog village.

A friend thet hain't in need is a friend indeed.

Atlas had a great reputation, but I'd like t' hev seen him try t' carry a mattress upstairs.

Figures dun't lie but you kin group 'em so they'll answer th' same purpose.

Laugh an' th' world laughs with you, weep an' it keeps on laughin'.

What's worse'n gittin' all scrooched down fer a pleasant evenin' at home an' then have a little son ask you t' give him a sentence containin' some word you never heard of?

A slice of eggplant makes a dandy sink stopper.

What comes easy goes easy—unless it's relatives.

Distant relatives er th' best kind, an' th' further th' better.

Johann Wolfgang Theophilus Mozart, the composer, died in December, 1792, at the age of thirty-six. While yet in his mother's arms young Mozart could and did play the accordion. At the age of four years he composed little airs that were quickly caught up and whistled broadcast. The sensibility of his organs appears to have been excessive—one bum note and he would slam the door and throw a fit on the lawn. The blast of a trombone was particularly irritating to him, invariably causing him to crawl under a bureau and there remain until the parade was out of sight. He was a marvelous piano player and easily the musical wonder of Europe. When a mere babe his father carried him about the country, exhibiting him and keeping the money. At Milan, 1770, an opera composed by Mozart at the age of fourteen was produced and given a run of twenty nights. He played the piano so constantly that his hands became useless when employed in any other way, consequently he was as much of a charge as an emotional actress.

THE GREAT AUK

"Little work has been done on the Greak Auk since the World War," explained Prof. Alex Tansey, o' School 43, Route 33, R.F.D., before a noonday luncheon o' the Mid-Continent Cement Block Association, at the New Palace hotel durin' the current year. "Many things have held back the work of assemblin' a complete skeleton o' this most interestin' prehistoric fowl. First, a lack o' funds, second, the new tariff bill, then the natural reaction follerin' in the wake of the uprisin' in India, an' a

THE GREAT AUK NEARING COMPLETION

general slump in scientific research attributable to a multiplicity o' things. It has required no end o' patience an' heroic work to reorganize an' crystallize any formidable amount of interest in the Great Auk, or Alk, or Awk, or Alck, or Alka, or Alky. The Great Auk covered an immense amount o' North America, it was a great prowler, an' parts necessary to a complete skeleton are widely scattered, a vertebra here, a spine there, etc. Try to find parts fer the ole Premier car an' you'll have some idea o' th' work necessary to erect a complete Great Auk. The parcels postage alone on parts so fer has reached a purty sum, an' shows no lettin' down. In assemblin' the neck alone thirty-four states contributed, the final joint arrivin' last week from Round-head, Ohio. The glacial period has held back the work. Many bones have come to light through diggin' fer hidden stills, an' street widen-in's. The beak o' th' skeleton o' which I speak wuz unearthed near Urbana, Ohio, where a farmer wuz settin' out a Andromeda Japonica, an' by the merest accident it fell into the hands of a passin' scientist who readily recognized it. Prob'ly many precious bones o' the Great Auk have been tossed aside by those unfamiliar with its chassis, an' general git up. The Great Auk belonged to the family Alcidae of which ther' wuz thirty-one species o' varyin' heights, but all were three-toed. The Great Auk wuz a nocturnal fowl, an' while it didn' fly nature provided it with the necessary arrangements to do so, as all connections wuz there ready in case of emergency. The correspondence in regard to assemblin' the Great Auk has been colossal, the costs o' railroad fares, expeditions, blind leads, an' gasoline, have been almost unbelievable. When the last bone is placed an' the skeleton o' the Great Auk is complete it'll mark the finish of one o' the greatest scientific undertakin's in all history, an' think of it, our own United States'll be the first to give to the world a skeleton o' the most astonishin' bird of which ther's any knowledge. Science, my friends, is a great thing. Most of us would be settin' around all week an' walkin' on Sunday if it wuzn' fer science."

PARCEL POST RULES

BY PUSTMASTER GABE CRAW

Pustmaster Gabe Craw has pusted th' followin' parcel pust rules an' regulations fer th' convenience o' th' patrons o' his office:

Th' fust zone shall include all territory within such quadrangle, in conjunction with every contiguous quadrangle, representin' an area havin' a mean radial distance o' approximately one hundred an' fifty miles from th' center o' a given unit o' area, er vice versa. A quadrangle is a four-sided figure.

* * *

Seventy-two inches is th' limit fer squashes.

* * *

Crosscut saws, porcupines an' scythes, an' other mailable matter o' a character likely, er liable, t' lacerate, maim, wound er otherwise interfere with a rural carrier's life, liberty er pursuit o' happiness should be carefully packed in excelsior an' crated.

* * *

All country butter held fer pustage'll be chloroformed after two days.

* * *

A goat muff should be deodorized an' mailed in a stove pipe, er other metal container.

* * *

When a pustal employee finds a message, er communication, either written er printed, secreted, hidden er allowed t' find lodgement in a sack o' p'taters, either sweet er Irish, er in any package, er container er sack containin' mailable merchandise, er merchandise offered fer mailin' under th' parcel pust laws, his fust duty shall be t' notify th' Third Assistant Pustmaster-General, givin' all th' circumstances, th' name o' th' sender, th' name o' th' addressee, date o' mailin' an' any other information that might interest th' department, whether directly er indirectly bearin' on th' case, after which he may go t' lunch.

THE END.

NOTE ON SOURCES

Chief sources:

Hubbard, Frank McKinney. Twenty-five annual books, 1906-1930.
———. Two collections, "Caricatures of Indiana Lawmakers and Lobbyists," 1903, 1905.
———. Essays in *American Magazine* and *Colliers*.
———. "Abe Martin," 1904–1930; "Short Furrows," 1911–1930; *Indianapolis News*, 1904–1930.
———. Two autobiographical sketches, *Indianapolis News*, Dec. 26, 1930; also tributes, expressions of sympathy, press comments, *Indianapolis News*, Dec. 26, 27, 1930.
Hubbard, Thomas. Collection of Kin Hubbard memorabilia; scrapbooks, family album, letters, theatrical programs and flyers. Thomas Hubbard, Editor and Publisher, *Bellefontaine Examiner* (the Hubbard family newspaper), Bellefontaine, Ohio.
Kelly, Fred C. *Kin Hubbard*. New York: Farrar, Straus and Young, 1952.
Rugenstein, John C. "Abe Martin Collection," Lilly Library, Indiana University.
Stillson, Blanche and Dorothy Risso. *Abe Martin–Kin Hubbard*. Indianapolis: Hoosier Bookshop, 1939.

Most of the material noted is in the Lilly Library, Indiana University, Bloomington, Indiana.

DAVID S. HAWES is Professor Emeritus of
Theatre and Drama at Indiana University.